RESOL 21ST CENTURY DISPUTES

BEST PRACTICES

FOR A FAST-PACED WORLD

GEOFF DRUCKER

PROSPECTA PRESS

Published by Prospecta Press

An imprint of Easton Studio Press

P.O. Box 3131

Westport, CT 06880

(203) 454-4454

www.prospectapress.com

Book and cover design by Barbara Aronica-Buck

Cartoons by DorianneArt (www.dorianneartstore.com)

Paperback Original ISBN: 978-1935212-74-4

E-book ISBN: 978-1-935212-73-7

FIRST EDITION

Printed in Canada

First printing: December 2011

MIX
Paper from
responsible sources
FSC® C004071

ANCIENT FOREST ™
FRIENDLY

TO MY WIFE, MICHELE WERNER,

whose unfailing support made this book possible

CONTENTS

PART IV: PUTTING IT ALL TOGETHER

ACKNOWLEDGMENTS

This journey started with mother, Emily Gindin, instilling an appreciation for good writing; my father, William Drucker, demonstrating how to convey complex information in simple terms (a valuable talent for an endocrinologist); and my stepfather, William Gindin, showing how to get points across through stories sweetened with a dash of humor (a critical skill for a trial lawyer).

It almost got derailed by acute myelogenous leukemia. The Virginia Hospital Center, the Memorial Sloan-Kettering Cancer Center, and the Leukemia and Lymphoma Society got me back on track. It is hard to write a book when you are dead—unless, of course, you are a celebrity.

The turning point was Mary Elcano's career advice: publish! Tina Adler and David Wilk helped steer me in the right direction, and Michael Shimkin, Barbara Fiorito, Joshua Shimkin, Dorianne Winkler, and Chuck Hirsch provided much needed help along the way.

The trail was blazed by the brilliant, creative, and dedicated social scientists whose research underlies this book.

Gail Werner, Karen Asaro, John McCammon, and Claudia Farr helped me scout out the ultimate destination by engaging with audiences prepublication.

My sincere thanks to all of you.

INTRODUCTION

It is in the minds of men, after all, that wars are spawned; to act upon the human mind, regardless of the issue or occasion for doing so, is to act upon the source of conflict and the potential source of redemption and reconciliation.

— James William Fulbright

When it comes to preventing and resolving disputes, our minds are outdated. They evolved to promote the survival of hunter-gatherers who lived in small, simple, homogeneous groups. The dynamic, diverse, interconnected world we live in presents dramatically different challenges and opportunities.

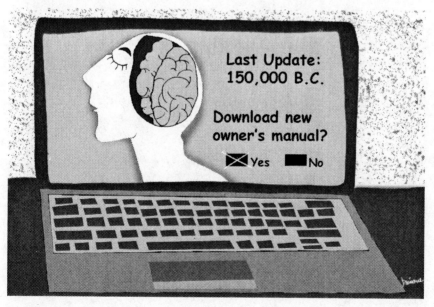

New mental software will take millions of years to develop.[1] In the meantime, you can vastly improve your ability to prevent and resolve disputes by learning more about Human Mind 1.0. Why is it ill-suited to 21st century disputes? How you can recognize and work around these shortcomings before trouble starts?

This book is about universals: thought processes shared by every mentally healthy person regardless of gender, age, race, ethnicity, culture, level of education, and other characteristics.[2] Differences do matter. Everyone is blessed with a unique blend of talents and inclinations. But as Maya Angelou has noted, "we are more alike, my friends, than we are unalike."[3] The traits we have in common play a far greater role in getting us into and out of disputes than the variations that set us apart.

Take this book personally. Keep asking yourself these questions:

- When has someone behaved this way toward me?
- When have I behaved this way toward someone else?
- How could I handle this type of situation differently if it happens again?

Keep practicing the skills you want to develop until they become second nature. No one has ever become a great golf, baseball, or tennis player simply by reading about how to swing a club, a bat, or a racquet. Mastery emerges from doing your best, noticing what is not working, adjusting accordingly, and vigorously weeding out bad habits—both old and new. Conflict resolution is no different. Education is the dawn of a lifetime journey.

For the sake of simplicity, I have illustrated concepts in this book with examples involving just two disputants. But all the best practices are scalable. Major disputes are typically referred to as being between groups, factions, organizations, or nations. But entities do not think; only people do. Conflicts exist solely within the minds of men and women. Whether just you and your manager are having a disagreement, or millions of people are at odds with each other, the thought processes in play are precisely the same.

PART I
THE BASICS

KEY TERMS

At the core of many disputes is a misunderstanding—a breakdown in communication. So let us begin by adopting a best practice for preventing this type of problem: defining essential words and phrases.

CONFLICT

Conflicts occur when people perceive that others are infringing on their **rights** or impeding their pursuit of **interests**. Thus, conflicts are extremely common, everyday occurrences. But we generally pay little or no attention to conflicts unless a significant right or interest is threatened and no easy resolution is in sight.

> At the beginning of their third date, Stan suggests a new Italian restaurant. Naomi says she'd prefer a Chinese place down the street.
>
> • Scenario #1: Stan and Naomi quickly agree to eat Italian tonight and Chinese next week.
>
> • Scenario #2: Stan becomes enraged, accuses Naomi of being a control freak who can't ever go along with what

someone else suggests, storms off, and never speaks to
her again.

Is this a conflict? Absolutely. Stan's desire to eat Italian impedes
Naomi's interest in eating Chinese, and vice-versa. Stan and Naomi do not
think of Scenario #1 as a conflict because they resolve it quickly and
agreeably. Both Stan and Naomi care far more about enjoying each other's
company than they do about what they eat. In Scenario #2, Stan prizes his
independence and feels Naomi is directly challenging this interest. His
reaction leaves no doubt that there is a conflict.

Right: a power or privilege to which someone is entitled by law or cus-
tom.

Interest: a need, want, or desire for something **material** or **social**.

Material: tangible or intangible property that fulfills, or aids in fulfilling, a physical need or desire.

- Food and shelter are tangibles that directly promote and safety.

- Seeds and tools are tangibles that assist in securing sustenance and
  safety.

- Money and information are intangibles that assist in fulfilling a variety of needs and wants.

Social: words or gestures that directly or indirectly indicate how one
person regards another.

- "I trust you," "I appreciate everything you have done," and "I respect
  your judgment," directly convey social meaning.

- Smiling, waving, or saying "You can count on me" indirectly conveys social meaning.

Causes of Conflict

Conflicts result from similarities, differences, and misunderstandings between people.

Similarity: the desire of two (or more) people for the same right or interest.

- Two children want to play with the same toy.

- Ten employees vie for the same promotion.

Difference: the desire of two (or more) people for rights and interests that interfere with each other.

- Law firm partners clash about how to attract and retain clients.

- Parents disagree on what school or camp is best for their child.

Misunderstanding: the mistaken belief that someone else is interfering with a person's pursuit of a right or interest.

- A patient believes a doctor is "just trying to cover his butt at my expense" by ordering several lab tests. The tests are necessary, but the doctor did not take the time to explain why.

- A girl is furious at her father for not showing up at her afternoon soccer game because, when he said "I'll be rooting for you" at breakfast, she thought he meant he would be there in person.

Conflict Resolution

A conflict is resolved when the people involved no longer perceive that someone else is infringing on their rights or impeding their interests. Perceptions change as a result of an action, a promise to act, or new information.

> A conflict arises when Hans, a security officer, refuses to let Imogene enter the building in which she works. Imogene wants to begin working, and Hans is interfering with her pursuit of this interest. The conflict could be resolved by
>
> - an action: Hans allows Imogene to enter.
>
> - a promise to act: Hans tells Imogene she may enter after signing in and presenting proper identification.
>
> - new information: Hans explains that the building may harbor toxic fumes from a recent fire. As a result, Imogene is no longer interested in entering.

People respond to conflicts in six different ways. Three are cooperative:

- **communication**: sharing information desired by another party

- **compromise**: giving up some of what you want in order to obtain the rest

- **collaboration**: working with the other party to pursue joint gains

The other three are competitive:

- **confrontation**: trying to defeat the other party

- **avoidance**: averting a confrontation

- **accommodation**: yielding to the other party's demands

Each strategy has its time and place. Communication (sharing information) is all that is needed when a conflict arises solely from miscommunication or a failure to communicate.[4] Compromise works best when a gain for one party necessarily results in a loss to the other (a "zero sum situation"); and both parties are better off settling for some of what they want than continuing to fight for the whole loaf. Collaboration is ideal when the parties can pursue their interests most effectively by working together.

Confrontation is best when you expect to emerge from battle victorious. Avoidance is the wisest course of action when you expect to lose. Accommodation is the only way out when you cannot avoid a losing battle or have already been defeated.

Disputants often employ more than one strategy simultaneously. War is the extreme case: soldiers cooperate devotedly with allies while competing viciously with enemies. In many peaceful situations as well, people blend cooperation and competition to advance their interests or exercise their rights. Strategies often shift over time as circumstances change and perceptions evolve. This is especially true in complex and protracted conflicts.

A cooperative strategy may fully resolve a conflict by addressing the rights and interests of all parties. A competitive strategy may resolve a conflict from the winner's standpoint, but not from the loser's. Many conflicts remain fully or partially unresolved. We frequently have to get by in life without having our rights respected or our interests met.

DISPUTE

A dispute arises when one or both parties to a conflict express, through words or gestures, that they perceive the other party as an impediment.

Many significant conflicts remain unexpressed because one or both parties fear a confrontation. An abused wife may tacitly go along with a decision her husband makes even though she disagrees with it. An associate in a law firm may put up with harassment from a senior partner to further his career. An uninsured patient may accept poor treatment and callous behavior from the staff in a medical clinic because she has nowhere else to turn. You cannot judge the degree of conflict by how much noise the parties are making. Fundamental disagreements often simmer quietly below the surface.

CHAPTER TWO

HOW THE HUMAN MIND WORKS: A BRIEF OVERVIEW

Since our brains—and only our brains—get us into and out of conflicts, we need to begin with a basic overview of how they react to events and make decisions.

THE UNCONSCIOUS MIND

Unconscious means involuntary. The unconscious mind automatically (1) controls bodily functions by sending and receiving signals through the nervous system, (2) molds input from the senses (sights, sounds, smells, tastes, and sensations) into perceptions; (3) preserves experiences as memories; and (4) melds perceptions and memories into emotions, which drive human behavior.[5]

Like every species, we have three essential needs:

Safety: protection against threats such as predators, diseases, and inhospitable conditions (e.g., extremes of heat, cold, dryness)

Sustenance: the fuel needed to function

Reproduction: creating another generation of sustainable life

Any species that fails to meet these needs goes extinct. Its DNA, the stuff of which life is made, dies out.

Most organisms protect, sustain, and reproduce themselves in pre-programmed (instinctive) ways. No thinking or choice is involved. Trees automatically bend toward the sun. Turtles automatically lay eggs on the beach where they were born. They cannot opt to do otherwise. To a great extent, we can control our actions because they are driven by emotions. Feelings push us to behave in certain ways, but we can resist these impulses. Thus, we generally act in ways that help us remain safe, sustain ourselves, and produce offspring not because we have to, but because we want to.

Emotional Breakdown

The vast array of human emotions can be broken down into a number of discrete categories. Actions that meet needs, or enhance our ability to meet needs, trigger positive emotions (pleasant feelings). Unmet needs, and actions that retard our ability to meet needs, trigger negative emotions (unpleasant sensations).

Material emotions tell us (a) what our needs are and (b) which actions will—or will not—fulfill them. We seek food and water to alleviate negative emotions of hunger and thirst—and to produce a positive emotion: satiation. We desire fresh meat and water because they are good sources of sustenance. We are repulsed by rancid meat and polluted water because they are bad (unsafe) sources of sustenance.

We strive for safety because tranquility and comfort are enjoyable, whereas fear and pain are not. We enjoy temperate, dry locations because they are healthy. We find frigid, damp, locations unpleasant because they threaten our well-being.

We seek to reproduce because sex feels great, and unfulfilled longing and frustration feel awful. Love for kin (children, parents, siblings, aunts, uncles, nieces, nephews) motivates us to nurture and protect those who

WHAT IS NATURAL?

Evolution is the survival of the fittest. But what makes a species fit? A competitive advantage, or a superior ability to live in harmony with other species? The answer is often both. Cooperation and competition are not mutually exclusive; many species blend the two. Two species with very different reputations, flowers and wolves, illustrate the point.

Flowers cooperate with birds and insects by providing sustenance (nectar) in exchange for assistance in reproducing (through the spread of pollen). But they compete with other flowers to attract birds and insects their way. Only the prettiest survive. Flowers too unsightly to entice spreaders of pollen fail to reproduce, and their DNA dies out.

Wolves cooperate with other pack members when hunting, but compete with each other for dominance. The relationship between a wolf pack and the individual elk it hunts is competitive: either the elk dies, or the pack goes hungry. The long-term relationship between a wolf pack and an elk herd, however, is cooperative. By preying on the sick and weak, wolves keep elk herds healthy and strong. A thriving elk herd provides a continuous source of food for wolves.[9] Like wolves, our ancestors secured food cooperatively because they could obtain more through teamwork than individual effort (while protecting each other from attack). They also cooperated in defending against warring tribes; raising their young; and caring for the sick, injured, and elderly. But our ancestors mimicked wolves by competing for positions of status within their clan and for the most desirable mates.

can pass along our DNA to future generations.[6] The closer the genetic match, the stronger the emotional bond. Love can, and often does, transcend biology, but, in general, the loss of a great aunt or a second cousin (who carry just a small fraction of our DNA) is not nearly as devastating as the loss of a son or daughter (who carry about half of our DNA).

EXAMPLES

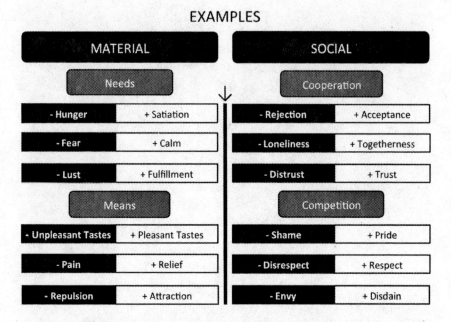

MATERIAL		SOCIAL	
Needs		**Cooperation**	
- Hunger	+ Satiation	- Rejection	+ Acceptance
- Fear	+ Calm	- Loneliness	+ Togetherness
- Lust	+ Fulfillment	- Distrust	+ Trust
Means		**Competition**	
- Unpleasant Tastes	+ Pleasant Tastes	- Shame	+ Pride
- Pain	+ Relief	- Disrespect	+ Respect
- Repulsion	+ Attraction	- Envy	+ Disdain

Social emotions guide us in meeting our needs by helping us act in concert with others. Humans are by no means the only species that survives through collective action. But our social relationships are far more diverse and complex than those of ants, sardines, rats, lions, bison, apes, and other communal animals because we have a much richer array of social emotions (and superior communication skills).[7]

Social emotions are both cooperative and competitive.[8] The former motivate us to form mutually beneficial relationships by treating others well and, therefore, ensuring others treat us well. The latter motivate us to outdo our peers.

Cooperative and competitive emotions are both positive and negative. We want to cooperate because its feels good when others are grateful and appreciative, and it feels bad when others reject us or regard us with contempt. We want to compete because we love to feel admired and respected and hate to feel jealous or envious.

Emotional Imbalance

The intensity and quantity of emotions are not evenly distributed between categories. Although everyone's range of feelings is unique, two characteristics are universal:

1. An emphasis on the negative

Since life is a constant struggle to survive—an endless succession of needs to fulfill—negative emotions are far more intense and long-lasting than their positive counterparts. If you are deprived of food for days, you will experience a gnawing, endless, all-consuming hunger. Thinking about anything else will be difficult. When it finally arrives, a decent meal will taste wonderful and provide a soothing feeling of fullness—but not for long. Other concerns will quickly push their way to the forefront. What other needs have you neglected while relentlessly searching for food? And where will you find the next decent meal?

People often tell themselves to focus on what they have, not what they lack, so they will be happier. But this is not how the mind works. Wired for survival, not happiness, it devotes most of its attention to what needs or wants are not being met.

2. More social than material

Social emotions—both negative and positive—greatly outnumber feelings regarding material needs.[10] We require just a few emotions to tell us what our fundamental needs are, and relatively few to indicate which activities will or will not help us sustain ourselves, remain safe, and reproduce. Most of our emotional palette is filled with sharp and subtle cues for navigating relationships.

Emotional Output

Material emotions drive us to address needs. When you are hungry, you feel like eating. When you are afraid you feel like getting out of danger.

Social emotions drive us to express feelings to others. We communicate primarily through a universal language of visual and vocal cues: facial expressions, body language, tones, and inflections. When you are happy you feel like smiling; when you are sad you feel like frowning. Anger inspires harsh tones; sympathy and concern inspire us to speak softly. We can and sometimes do convey emotions through words (e.g., "Wow, that's surprising!"), but language cannot fully capture the pathos of a cold stare or a warm embrace.[11]

CONSCIOUS MIND

The voluntary part of the mind controls language, reasoning, decision making, and the execution of decisions. It verbalizes (forms concepts into words) in order to reason (think). It reasons in order to decide (make choices). It executes decisions in order to meet needs. The conscious mind also uses language to share thoughts and feelings with other people.

The choices we make are about how best to fulfill a drive and how to resolve internal conflicts between competing drives.[12] Many internal conflicts are between short-term impulses and long-term desires:[13]

When her perennially disorganized manager, Dwight, shows up late for a meeting that he called and then asks, "Okay, so what is this about?" Jill is infuriated. But to keep her relationship with Dwight on track, Jill does her best to act nonchalant.

Janis is extremely excited: 123 Oak Street is the perfect house for her. But she hopes the seller will drop the price. So when Richard, the seller's agent, asks what she thinks, Janet pretends to be only mildly interested.

Due to a long flight delay, Steven arrives in Los Angeles hungry and exhausted. But he pushes through a full morning of meetings in order to keep an important project moving forward.

Jill and Janis suppress short-term social emotions—fury and excitement—to further long-term goals. Steven suppresses material emotions —hunger and fatigue—for the same reason.*

Suppressing an impulse means either dictating the time, place, and manner in which it is expressed; or delaying action until the impulse weakens or disappears. Jill can decide to take out her fury at the gym later in the afternoon, complain to her boyfriend at dinner, or just wait until she gets another job and no longer cares about Dwight's shortcomings.

Because emotions arise unconsciously, we cannot control what we feel.[14] This division of labor between the two minds is essential for survival. If we could consciously select emotions, we would chose to feel happy regardless of whether our needs were being met.**

Because our feelings are attuned to the rhythms of a long-gone era, they often goad us in the wrong direction.[15] Strong willpower (emotional control) is therefore critical for preventing and resolving disputes.

* Health is a key component of safety, and rest is critical for health.

** This is one of the reasons why mood-altering drugs can be lethal. They provide a degree of control over feelings that is denied to us by nature.

PART II
THE UNCONSCIOUS MIND

CHAPTER THREE

IDENTITY

Tell all the Truth but tell it slant—
Success in Circuit lies
Too bright for our infirm Delight
The Truth's superb surprise
As Lightening to the Children eased
With explanation kind
The Truth must dazzle gradually
Or every man be blind—

— Emily Dickinson

To meet our needs, we must convince others to help us. We accomplish this by developing and maintaining a positive identity—that is, a reputation for providing material value (useful goods, services, or information) and/or social value (companionship, love, appreciation, respect, reliability).[16]

Two innate (hard-wired) rules guide the quest for a positive identity: **reciprocity**—seeking fairness (balance) in relationships—and **self-promotion**—interpreting information self-servingly.

This chapter explains how these rules mold behavior and what happens when their paths cross.

RECIPROCITY

Our innate sense of fairness[17] generates the following emotions:

Action	Response
I provide a benefit.	I feel entitled to receive equal value.
I receive a benefit.	I feel obligated to return equal value.
I do inadvertent harm.	I feel obligated to provide compensation equal to the harm done.
Someone inadvertently harms me.	I feel entitled to compensation equal to the harm done.
I sacrifice for someone's benefit.	I feel they should sacrifice equally.
Someone sacrifices for my benefit.	I feel obligated to sacrifice equally.
I do intentional harm.	I feel I should apologize or be punished in proportion to the magnitude of the offense.
Someone intentionally harms me.	I feel entitled to an apology or to revenge proportional to the magnitude of the offense.

Since these emotions drive but do not compel behavior, people can, and often do, override them—a subject we will return to later.

Key Characteristics

Reciprocity is to social bonding as gravity is to physical bonding: the guiding force behind every relationship.

1. Universal
The unconscious mind regards every encounter with another human being as an exchange of value and gauges whether it seems fair. Some exchanges are explicit: a vendor sells a doughnut for seventy-five cents. But most are implicit: the participants do not regard their interaction as

an exchange and do not discuss or think in terms of value changing hands.

> Bob says hello to his neighbor, Macon, as he walks by.
> Macon says hello back.

This is an exchange of recognition. If Macon did not say hello back and grimaced instead, Bob would feel slighted because he gave more social value than he received.

> Amy listens attentively while Grace talks about her problems. Then Grace listens attentively as Amy recounts what is happening in her life.

This is an exchange of concern. If Grace had abruptly ended the conversation as soon as Amy began talking about herself, Amy would have felt disrespected.

> Sandy works several nights and weekends, unpaid, while Doris is ill. When Doris returns, she tells Sandy how much she appreciates her efforts.

This is an exchange of material value (service) for social value (appreciation). In the short term, a sincere "thanks" is all Sandy needs to feel the exchange is fair. But six months from now, if Sandy comes down with the flu, she will be outraged if Doris refuses to cover for her.

2. Perpetual

The unconscious mind regards every interaction as part of an ongoing relationship. Why? Hunter-gatherers lived in small communities in which everyone engaged with everyone else over and over again. There were no casual encounters. If you cheated a member of your clan, then, in addition to demanding retribution or seeking revenge, she would warn others not to trust you. If you allowed another clan member to cheat you, she would not only soon attempt to exploit you again; she would also curry favor with others by letting them know you are an easy target. Thus, to survive, our forbearers needed emotions that drove them to right every wrong by securing equal value or meting out equal punishment.[18]

3. Relative

The unconscious mind assesses fairness in relative, not absolute, terms.[19] Relative to what? To others who are similarly situated. Is it fair for a landlord to charge $2,000 per month for a windowless studio apartment? Yes, if similar studios typically rent for that much or more. No, if luxury three-bedroom apartments typically rent for $1,800 per month. Is it fair for Joshua to ask his sister, Harriet, to spend all her vacation time caring for their aging mother? Yes, if Joshua is spending all his vacation time this way. No, if Joshua if spending all his free time skiing.

4. Subjective

Fairness is in the eye of the beholder. Whether an exchange seems equal depends entirely on how someone views the world and from what vantage point they view it from.[20]

What is similar?

Is a bottle of Chianti fair compensation for a bottle of Riesling? To someone who does not like wine or does not consume alcohol, one bottle is just as good as another. To a connoisseur, the bottles may be as different as night and day.

Is a plaque on the wall of a hospital fair compensation for $10,000? A destitute victim of malpractice would regard the exchange as completely unfair. A multimillionaire whose life was miraculously saved would regard it as a great deal.

5. Cumulative

We judge fairness based on the total amount of material and social value furnished and received, not just on a single component. An apology (social value) may be combined with a check (material value) to compensate

WHO IS SIMILARLY SITUATED?

Kevin, the child of a single mother on welfare, earns the same high-school grades and achievement test scores as Grady, the child of two professional parents. Should a college admissions office treat Kevin and Grady alike or prefer Kevin because he appears to have overcome greater challenges?

Clara, a physician, and Marcos, a physician's assistant, work in the same clinic and perform the same procedures with the same degree of skill. Should Clara and Marcos receive the same pay, or does Clara deserve more because her education and training are superior?

Kahlil, a fighter pilot, and Maureen, the navigator of a drone (a remotely controlled aircraft), destroy equally valuable targets in a key battle. Should they be honored equally, or does Kahlil deserve more recognition because he put his life at risk?

There are no objectively right or wrong answers to these questions. Reasonable minds can and do disagree about what is fair.

for a loss. A technician may charge a single price for both fixing a computer (material value) and furnishing information about how to avoid future computer problems (another form of material value).

How Identity Affects Reciprocity

The more positively you are regarded by others—that is, the more they think you have to offer—the more they will provide in return. When two people view each other positively, their imaginations are the only limit on how they can cooperate for mutual gain. Exchanges of material value are the easiest to

IS THERE A BETTER WAY?

Reciprocity—tit for tat—is the simplest rule imaginable. Could a more sophisticated regime produce a higher degree of cooperation? So far, the answer is no. Attempts to improve on reciprocity using advanced computer technology have all come up short. Why? Simplicity is an asset, not a liability. It makes consequences crystal clear.[21]

This is why, since ancient times, laws and customs designed to promote cooperation have all been based on reciprocity. To cite just two well-known examples, the Golden Rule teaches us to do unto others as we would have them do unto us,[22] and the Bible warns that "whatsoever a man soweth, that shall he also reap."[23]

Today, we rely on reciprocity (operating under the name "mutually assured destruction") to deter the ultimate conflict: a nuclear war. The belief that those who sow annihilation will reap annihilation deters leaders from starting down the path to Armageddon.

understand. If John has more fruit than he can consume before it rots, and Sarah has more meat than she can eat before it turns bad, it makes sense for John to trade fruit to Sarah in exchange for meat. Social value is less obvious. Why would anyone willingly trade something of clear tangible value, such as food or medicine, for mere words or gestures, such as a "thank you" or a hug? Because social value (how you are regarded by others) is a medium of exchange akin to paper money. It has no intrinsic value (innate worth) but it creates expectations that can be exchanged for goods or services at a later date. And woe to those who fail to meet social obligations. If Sally does a favor for Steven, all she may immediately receive in return is appreciation. But when he thanks Sally, Steven tacitly acknowledges that he now owes her a favor. So when the opportunity arises, Steven feels obligated to help Sally, and Sally expects Steven to be there for her.

Reliability (trust) is critical because it signals you will live up to expectations. If you are distrusted, others will cooperate only if you provide value first (or simultaneously) and they can easily verify that you performed as promised. For example, you do not need to trust a street vendor in order to purchase a *New York Times* from him. You can grab a paper right before you pay, and you easily distinguish it from another newspaper. But if you are purchasing an airline ticket, trust in the carrier's ability to deliver you safely on a future date is essential.

How Reciprocity Affects Identity

Reputations are based on how much value people can command. An artist develops a much better reputation if his paintings quickly sell for $1 million than if they linger in galleries unsold. A lawyer develops a much better reputation if she has clients lining up to pay her $750 an hour than if she cannot attract business charging $150 an hour.

Reputations (identities) spread because one of the most common forms of exchange in all societies is information about who has what to offer.[24] The reason is simple: acquiring this information through dialogue is far more efficient than learning it through trial and error. Imagine Rebecca needs a nanny for her three-month-old daughter. To locate one on her own, she would have to place an advertisement, interview numerous candidates, and try out the top ones for a few days under close supervision. Instead, Rebecca e-mails a few friends. Sarah promptly writes back with contact information for Jolene, a colleague at work whose youngest child is about to enter first grade. Jolene tells Rebecca that her nanny, Mia, is looking for work and is first rate. Problem solved. Although the parties involved do not think of their networking as a series of transactions, here is what they exchanged:

- Sarah helps Rebecca find a nanny, so Rebecca now owes Sarah a favor.

- Jolene helps Mia find another employer, so Mia now owes Jolene a favor.

It is through such sharing of information that identities, both positive and negative, spread far and wide.

EXAMPLES OF EXCHANGES

Material Value for Material Value
- **Barter:** Parties exchange goods, services, or information: one pound of meat for two pounds of grain.
- **Trade:** One party provides a good or service; the other provides a medium of exchange: One pound of meat for eight dollars.
- **Restitution:** One party provides goods or services equal to the amount of loss suffered by the other party: A new saw comparable to one that someone borrowed and broke.

Material Value for *Social Value*
- **Gifts, favors, and donations:** One party provides material value and receives social value in return: (1) Someone who has been ill thanks a friend for providing care. (2) A mother pays for her son's college tuition and receives gratitude in return.

Social Value for *Social Value*
- **Apologies and forgiveness:** (1) After negligently breaking a prized bow he borrowed, a hunter apologizes and promises to be more careful. The person whose bow was broken forgives the hunter. (2) A daughter apologizes to her mother after losing her temper and promises to be more respectful. The mother forgives the daughter.
- **Displays of mutual respect:** (1) One person wishes another a nice day. The other person repeats this wish. (2) One person compliments another on her hair or dress. The other person says something complimentary in return.

Combinations of Value
- An apology (social value) and partial restitution (material value).
- One pound of grain now (present value) and a promise to provide two pounds after the harvest (future value).
- An agreement to dig a new well (material value) and to carefully ration the water acquired from it (a material sacrifice).

Reciprocity and Conflict

Reciprocity—our innate sense that human relationships should be fair—is the root cause of both cooperation and conflict. It promotes cooperation by encouraging us to engage in balanced, mutually beneficial exchanges. It promotes conflict by prodding us to even things out whenever an exchange seems to be tipped in the other party's favor.

If a conflict results from a misunderstanding, all that may be required to resolve it is communication. If one party convinces the other that the exchange was fair, the conflict disappears.

If, through communication, one party convinces the other that an exchange was unfair, the party in the wrong can resolve the conflict by providing an agreed-upon amount of material value (e.g., money) or social value (e.g., an apology).

If the parties cannot agree on what is fair, then one or both will feel compelled to even the score. But it will never seem even to both. If

HOW APOLOGIES WORK

The wrongdoer (1) conveys regret and remorse commensurate with the amount of damage done, and (2) promises not to harm the victim again.

By acknowledging that a victim deserves fair treatment, an apology restores the respect the victim lost by being wronged.

When a victim forgives the wrongdoer, she indicates that (1) the wrongdoer's display of regret and remorse was sincere,[25] and (2) the wrongdoer's promise to behave well in the future is credible. In other words, forgiveness signals that the wrongdoer can once again be trusted.*

---

* An apology may be valuable even if it does not come close to restoring or creating a cooperative relationship. Imagine that a forty-two-year-old drug addict with an extensive rap sheet kills a seven-year-old girl while driving under the influence of narcotics. An apology cannot possibly compensate for this horrible loss, but it may provide a grieving family some measure of comfort.

ALTRUISM

For cultural reasons, people frequently pretend not to care whether their contributions to others are recognized or rewarded. We may be loath to admit it, but our minds lack an impulse to sacrifice and receive nothing in return. Reciprocity is what brings out the best in us.[26]

This point is best illustrated through an extreme example: a patriotic citizen volunteers for military service and then, in the heat of battle, risks his life to protect other members of his unit. Isn't this the epitome of selflessness? Note that this brave soldier receives two forms of value in exchange. First, should the need arise, his comrades will put their lives on the line to save him. In warfare, solid bonds improve everyone's odds of survival because a cohesive unit is less likely to suffer casualties than one fractured by distrust and disrespect. This is why warriors quickly ostracize anyone who fails to display an appropriate esprit de corps. Paradoxically, risking life and limb for others is an excellent strategy for staying alive.[27] Second, in recognition of willingly enduring hardship and risk, soldiers receive highly esteemed medals, promotions, honors, and privileges. Generally speaking, the greater the accomplishment, the greater the reward.

When the brave defend the weak, the wealthy aid the poor, or the healthy care for the sick, we feel their efforts should be repaid with corresponding amounts of appreciation precisely because we do not expect people to be selfless. We recognize that if their bravery, philanthropy, or compassion is ignored, they will be less inclined to help in the future; and others will hesitate to follow in their footsteps for fear their good deeds will also go unrequited.*

We do not live in a perfect world in which every sacrifice is appropriately recognized. But the fact that we think people should always get as good as they give—even if their compensation comes solely in the form of gratitude—demonstrates that reciprocity lies at the root of generosity.

---

* Honoring the dead encourages the living to risk making the ultimate sacrifice for their community.

Raymond exacts revenge on Solomon, Solomon will think he was treated unjustly and, therefore, feel compelled to exact revenge on Raymond. Confrontation tends to resolve a conflict from the standpoint of one party while triggering conflict from the standpoint of another. Only through a meeting of the minds can a dispute be resolved to the satisfaction of all.

SELF-PROMOTION

We enhance our identity by creating a positive self-image and then leveraging this image to obtain value from others.

Step 1: Creating a Positive Self-Image

The unconscious mind favorably interprets information it perceives as a reflection on identity.[28] This includes not only personal behavior and characteristics, but also people, groups, property, and ideas associated with an individual's self-image.[29]

- Parents commonly perceive their children's accomplishments as an indicator of their own status and, consequently, exaggerate their children's abilities and achievements.[30]

- Employees commonly perceive the organization they work for as a mark of their status, especially if they occupy a senior position, so they are prone to have an inflated sense of its value and effectiveness.

- Landowners commonly perceive their home as a reflection of their self-image, so they tend to have a disproportionate sense of its beauty and worth.[31]

MORE THAN 100 PERCENT

Here is a small sample of results from studies on the self-serving bias.*

Personal Qualities:

- 94 percent of Americans consider themselves at least slightly above average in terms of honesty.
- 89 percent rate themselves above the norm in common sense.
- Well over two-thirds place themselves in the top half with regard to friendliness, intelligence, physical appearance, and health.[34]

Other People:

95 percent of people who identify themselves as "in love" believe their partner is above average in looks, intelligence, warmth, and sense of humor.[35]

Groups:

In making personal investment decisions, over 50 percent of Fortune 500 chief executive officers overvalue the companies they run.[36]

Property:

Owners typically believe the appropriate sale price is twice what prospective buyers think is fair to pay.[37]

Ideas:

- Parties in final offer arbitration (in which the decision maker makes an either/or choice between proposals) overestimate the odds of their offer being selected by an average of 18 percent.
- Although only 33 percent of new firms survive longer than five years, over 80 percent of entrepreneurs rate their odds of success as 70 percent or better, and 33 percent are "certain" they will succeed.[38]

---

* For a sampling of other research on self-promotion, see Michael Shermer, Science of Good and Evil: Why People Cheat, Gossip, Care, Share, and Follow the Golden Rule (New York: Times Books, 2004), 178. One study revealed that people who engage in behaviors that carry a negative social stigma, such as adultery and tax evasion, justify their behavior by overestimating the number of other people who behave in a similar fashion.

- Executives commonly perceive the ideas they advance as markers of their competence, so they have an abundance of faith in their wisdom and utility.

The unconscious mind also promotes and protects a positive self-image by negatively interpreting information about individuals, groups, and ideas that threaten identity. The less regard we have for them, the higher regard we can have for ourselves.[32] For example, imagine that whenever Katherine speaks up at a team meeting, Daniel shoots her down, coldly dismissing her suggestions as "naïve" or "ludicrous." If Katherine views Daniel as a genius whose sole motivation is to aid the team, she must see herself as a stubborn imbecile. If Katherine perceives Daniel as a destructive moron, she can think of herself as bright and irrepressible.

To what extent does the unconscious mind bend, twist, or ignore reality? That depends on the circumstances. The further the truth departs from the image it feels compelled to protect, the more the mind distorts reality.[33]

Step 2: Leveraging a Positive Self-Image

A positive self-image aids in forming cooperative relationships (negotiating) because the more you think you have to offer, the more you deem fair to demand in return. And the more you demand, the more you are likely to get. Studies consistently show that negotiators who aim high obtain better results than those with more modest aspirations.[39] Why? Negotiators generally have limited information about what the other party has to offer. Convince someone they will gain a lot from you, and they will be happy to pay you handsomely.

A positive self-image helps in competition by fueling ambition and resilience. We pursue goals we think are within reach and steer clear of struggles we regard as hopeless. So self-confidence is a self-fulfilling prophecy. People who think they can win persist until they do.[40] People lacking in self-confidence either never step up to the starting line, or they give up partway when they encounter obstacles they do not believe they can overcome.

Drawbacks to Self-Promotion

1. Overreaching. Demanding negotiators get more when a deal is struck, but they run a greater risk of failing to reach an agreement. When you ask for more, you may get more; however, another possibility is that the other side will regard your demands as unreasonable and refuse to cooperate.[41]

In competition, self-confidence boosts performance but does not guarantee victory. An opponent may be equally confident, and with better

SELF-DECEPTION VS. DELIBERATE LYING

With respect to lying, ignorance (self-deception) is truly bliss because it makes you more credible.[45] Since one of the most important decisions we make is who to trust, our minds are adept at detecting conscious lies.[46] There are several telltale signs:

Nervousness and ambivalence: When people know they are lying, they recognize the risk of getting caught and worry about the consequences. Moral qualms may also produce anxiety, hesitancy, or uncertainty.

Difficulty speaking: Consciously fabricating a consistent and credible story that achieves a particular objective is difficult. So is memorizing the story in case it has to be repeated.* Thus, liars tend to speak abnormally slowly. They cannot think fast enough to keep up with their normal rate of speech. In addition, they tend to stumble over words, make errors in grammar or syntax, blink, or stutter abnormally because they are so focused on what they are saying that they cannot pay sufficient attention to how they are saying it. →

* As Mark Twain once remarked, "If you tell the truth you don't have to remember anything."

reason. An inflated self-image sometimes leads people to fight battles they would be better off avoiding.[42]

2. Overestimating. Distorted memories teach the wrong lessons. When we ignore or minimize faults, we fail to learn from them and are condemned to repeat mistakes.[43]

3. Offending. When distorted memories lead people to claim too much credit for successes and heap too much blame on others for failures, they trigger conflicts.[44]

→ **Inappropriate affect:** When people state what they believe to be true, their tone of voice and body language naturally align with their verbal message. Kind words, if sincerely meant, are delivered with a soft tone and open gestures. Angry words, if they convey the speaker's true feelings, are harshly delivered with closed or hostile gestures. Deliberate liars must mask their true feelings and feign the tone and gestures that match their words. This is even more difficult than inventing a credible story.[47] So when words and emotional cues (tone of voice and body language) seem misaligned, we naturally place much more stock in the emotional cues.[48]

If you firmly believe your words are the God's honest truth (even though they are not):

- You have no cause for concern that others won't believe you, or that you are behaving immorally or unethically.
- You can speak normally because you are merely recalling data from memory, not trying to edit it to suit your purposes.
- Your affect naturally aligns with your words.

In short, the more thoroughly you deceive yourself, the better you come across to others.

The two scenarios that follow illustrate how self-deception works in practice. "The Bottom Line" shows how the unconscious mind distorts reality. "Webscan" shows how these distortions can either help or hurt, depending on how the other party responds.

THE BOTTOM LINE

Part 1: Casting Blame

Two months ago, Jason Brickman took over from his father, Howard, as manager of Roland Jessup's fleet of sportfishing boats. Howard retired after managing the fleet for thirty-five years.

Jason receives a small salary and a percentage of the net profit from the six boats currently in the fleet. The expenses of running an aging fleet have risen significantly over the past few years, driving the net profit down 25 percent.

Melinda, Jason's wife, used to earn a good salary as a teacher, but she resigned last year to care full-time for their two-year-old son, who has autism. Melinda and Jason are treading water financially by running up credit card debt.

Two days ago, just at the peak of tourist season, Miguel Dominguez, who has captained the Bottom Line since Howard Brinkman hired him thirty years ago, warned Jason that the engine was dying and recommended decommissioning the ship immediately. Miguel reminded Jason that he had mentioned the need for repairs at their two prior meetings. Jason reminded Miguel of the company's financial situation and said there'd be plenty of time to rebuild the engine during the winter.

Yesterday, an engine fire on the Bottom Line injured two crew members. Passengers described the fire as "raging" and said the ship was "in peril" before the Coast Guard arrived.

Step 1: Preserving a Positive Self-Image

Jason's unconscious mind minimizes his role by

- emphasizing Miguel's prerogative as captain of the Bottom Line to have refused to set sail if he felt the ship was not seaworthy;

- ignoring the pressure he put on Miguel to keep the ship operating;

- disregarding Miguel's prior warnings about the engine's poor condition; and

- assuming crew members were below deck because they were loafing off and, therefore, have only themselves to blame.[49]

Jason also discounts his range of choices by

- emphasizing his fiduciary duty to make the Bottom Line profitable; and

- characterizing the fire as a fluke that could not possibly have been predicted.

Finally, Jason minimizes the outcome by

- presuming the injured crew members magnified their injuries to secure workers' compensation and time off; and

- presuming the sportfishermen on board (who are notorious for telling tall tales) exaggerated the extent of the blaze and the danger it caused to wow the crowd at the bar that night and their buddies back home.[50]

Step 2: Leveraging a Positive Self-Image
When Roland confronts him, Jason explains why others were to blame for the accident, why decommissioning the ship was not a realistic option, and why the damage was minimal. Will Roland buy this story and allow

Jason to retain his identity as a fleet manager? That is unclear; self-deception is not a panacea. It is clear, however, that coming across as confident and sincere improves Jason's chances of keeping his job.

But by casting blame on Miguel and the crew rather than himself, Jason increases his odds of making the same mistake again (substituting his judgment for Miguel's). He also puts himself at odds with Miguel, who no doubt recalls the events leading up to the accident very differently.

Part 2: Reeling in Glory

Imagine that on that fateful day when Miguel recommended decommissioning the Bottom Line, the engine's worn parts somehow managed to keep chugging. A competitor's vessel, however, ran aground in a thick fog and started sinking. After thirty-five years of navigating these coastal waters, Miguel knew he could find his way blindfolded. So despite the danger, which kept other vessels away, Miguel immediately responded to the distress call and rescued the ship's crew and passengers just in the nick of time.

Like the proverb says, "Success has 100 parents, failure is an orphan." Whereas "Casting Blame" illustrates how Jason attempts to distance himself from a major failure, "Reeling in Glory" provides Jason an opportunity to claim a success as his brainchild.

Step 1: Enhancing a Positive Self-Image

Jason's unconscious mind seizes the opportunity to inflate his status by

- highlighting his **role** in facilitating the rescue by keeping the Bottom Line in service;

- emphasizing his **range of choice** (he could have listened to Miguel and decommissioned the Bottom Line); and

- pumping up the **outcome** by noting that, in addition to saving precious lives, the daring rescue secured favorable publicity for the Bottom Line.[51]

Step 2: Leveraging a Positive Self-Image

When describing the daring rescue to Roland and other members of the seafaring community, Jason characterizes it as a personal triumph—vivid proof of his uncanny ability to make the right decision at the right time. Overconfidence in his decision-making ability, however, may lead Jason to take unwarranted risks in the future. And claiming credit for the rescue puts him at odds with Miguel, who no doubt feels he deserves the accolades.

WEBSCAN

Part 1: Winning in Competition

Amanda and Ravi manage separate marketing teams within Transnat, a large electronics manufacturer. When the chief marketing officer, Steven, launches a new hybrid product, WebScan, Amanda and Ravi both lobby for their team to take the lead on marketing. Steven invites them to submit competing proposals and present their ideas at an executive committee meeting.

Thoroughly convinced that she can create an enormous international market for WebScan within six months, Amanda exudes confidence during her presentation. Captivated by her polish and enthusiasm, the executive committee puts Amanda in charge of marketing WebScan and doubles her budget and staff. Ravi congratulates Amanda and offers his full support.

Why does the executive committee take Amanda's attitude into account? Because people who believe they will succeed are more likely to achieve their objectives than people who expect to fail. The same logic explains why employers favor applicants who believe they have what it takes to meet or exceed expectations; investment bankers prefer loaning to entrepreneurs who are optimistic about their business plans; and voters select candidates for public office who exude confidence.

Part 2: Competing Foolishly

Now let us change the facts: while the executive committee was highly impressed by Amanda's presentation, Ravi came across as equally confident and better qualified.

A few days later, as she was anxiously awaiting word back from the executive committee, the following message from a friend popped up on Amanda's Blackberry: "Hey, Ravi just asked me to work on his WebScan team. Okay with you? Thought this was going to be your big gig??" Amanda was devastated. Convinced that the executive committee, composed of six men and two women (one of whom was traveling during the meeting) must have been biased, Amanda retained an attorney, Jessica, to sue for sex discrimination.

It was not foolish of Amanda to compete with Ravi for control of WebScan marketing. In some contexts, the loser gets points for trying hard and putting up a good fight. But when overconfidence leads Amanda to rule out the possibility that Ravi won on merit, she lands herself in an uphill court battle with Transnat.

In addition to being a very significant cause of litigation, inflated egos induce entrepreneurs to start businesses they are ill-equipped to launch, goad managers into pursuing projects they lack the wherewithal to complete, and suck politicians into wars their country lacks the resources or will to win.[52]

Part 3: Securing Favorable Terms

Six months after filing suit, Jessica meets with Transnat's attorney, Stan, to discuss settlement. Jessica knows she does not have a lot of facts to work with, but she has great faith in her ability to persuade a jury. So Jessica estimates she has a 40 percent chance of winning and predicts a jury will award $200,000 in damages (in light of the bonus Ravi received). Thus, Jessica insists on a settlement in the $50,000–$100,000 range.

Stan argues that a $10,000 "nuisance value" settlement would be more appropriate. Jessica refuses to budge and passionately argues the merits of her client's case. Stan eventually caves in and agrees to pay $75,000.

Here we see self-confidence providing a distinct edge in negotiating. When lawyers try to iron out the terms of a settlement, they define fairness in relation to the probable outcome at trial. If the chances of a jury awarding the plaintiff (suing party) $1 million are 99 percent, it is fair for the defendant to pay a lot of money. If the plaintiff's chances are 1 percent, a far more modest settlement is in order. By displaying confidence in her ability to prevail, Jessica convinces Stan to put significantly more money on the table.

Could Jessica have feigned confidence even though she believed her case was a loser? Sure. And, had she done so, she would not have been the first lawyer in history to bluff her way to victory. However, people sound more credible when they believe what they are saying. (See Self-Deception vs. Deliberate Lying, pages 32–33.) Thus lawyers are just as prone as everyone else to convince themselves that their self-serving viewpoint is accurate.

Part 4: Impasse

Let us change the facts one more time: instead of caving into Jessica's demands, Stan comes on just as strong, insisting his chances of prevailing are 95 percent. He is every bit as confident in his trial skills as Jessica and has better facts to work with. Transnat has a good track record in promoting female employees, and although Ravi is younger and less experienced than Amanda, his performance evaluations were stellar. So Stan sticks to his guns and lets Jessica walk out.

If—as is very often the case—both sides overestimate their chances of success in competition, they will fail to see eye-to-eye on what constitutes a fair settlement. Jessica thinks she has a 40 percent chance of winning; Stan puts her odds at 5 percent. So they cannot agree on a settlement number.

When this case goes to trial, won't one of the attorneys become the victor? Not really. The jury will rule in one side's favor, but that does not mean that the "winning" side will have improved its position by turning down a reasonable settlement and going to trial. Some competitions are win-win because the "loser" gains more by competing than she would have by avoiding a confrontation. "Winning in Competition" (page 37) exemplifies this point. By competing vigorously and accepting defeat graciously, Ravi raises his profile with senior management and positions himself for the next choice assignment.

Unfortunately, competitions more frequently are lose-lose because victory is more costly to the winner than an available compromise. Courts are great repositories of lose-lose conflicts because of the costs to both parties in time, money, and aggravation.[53] As Voltaire observed, "I've been ruined twice in my life; once when I lost in litigation, and once when I won." Battles between family members, ethnic and religious groups, and nations often yield lose-lose outcomes as well.

In summary, by helping us compete and negotiate effectively, self-promotion improves our identity in most situations. But it sometimes diminishes our prospects by prodding us to reject sound agreements or fight counter-productive battles.

WHEN RECIPROCITY AND SELF-PROMOTION COLLIDE

Our minds mediate a never-ending battle between competitive and cooperative emotions.[54] We want to get and do not want to give. But we know we should give as much as we receive. We need both sets of emotions to survive. "Wants" tell us what we need. "Shoulds" tell us how to get it.

Conflicts arise when we yield to temptation by knowingly taking more than we deserve or returning less than we owe. They also arise when we unknowingly (unconsciously) demand too much or provide too little because we view the world through a self-serving lens.

These two causes of conflict, conscious greed and unconscious self-promotion, surely have been around since the dawn of mankind. But they now operate in a profoundly different context.

21ˢᵀ CENTURY CHALLENGES

Our emotions are attuned to the needs of people who live in small groups and have a single, stable identity; share a common body of knowledge; adhere to traditional practices for airing differences; and interact with each other repeatedly.

This is not how we live today.

Challenge #1: Narrow, Fixed Views

How often have you spoken or heard one of the following phrases in a situation that was anything but life threatening?

"No way! . . . I can't be wrong about this! . . . That couldn't have happened! . . . This cannot be! . . . There has to be some other explanation!"

"I cannot admit defeat! . . . This is a must-win situation!"

What makes people feel they need to shield themselves from the truth? Our ancestors had a single, static identity: a fixed role (based on age and gender) within one group. Those who failed to live up to expectations were banished (ostracized).* Operating on the edge of survival, hunter-gatherers could not afford to carry anyone who refused to follow the accepted norms of behavior.

---

* We punish in much the same way today—just not as harshly. People who engage in anti-social behavior are banished to jails and prisons. Prisoners who misbehave are banished to solitary confinement. Children who misbehave are banished to time-out.

Banishment was a death sentence. Our ancestors could not live independently and stood little chance of being taken in by another tribe or clan. Thus, when accused of behaving in a manner that was inconsistent with their role, people had no choice but to dig in their heels and mount a vigorous defense. Bending, twisting, or denying facts could be a lifesaver.

Powerful negative emotions fueled this defense. Nothing causes more profound sorrow, devastation, or emptiness than being abandoned, disrespected, or disregarded by the people you most value.[55] Isolation and loneliness trigger the depths of despair. These experiences are called "heartbreaking" because they feel like a massive physical blow.[56] People will go to extraordinary lengths to avoid such pain.

Modern identities are complex and dynamic.[57] They are complex because they consist of a myriad of different affiliations including family relationships, community organizations, religious congregations, schools, alumni associations, social clubs, workplaces, professional associations, charitable organizations, political parties, and informal personal and professional networks. Some of these affiliations overlap—we interact with the same people in different contexts—and some do not. Modern identities are dynamic because affiliations come and go as circumstances and interests change. Thanks to modern technology, affiliations are not limited by geography; you can develop and maintain a relationship with anyone on the planet who has Internet access.

As a result, we can (a) gain cooperation from members of numerous groups, (b) add value in a wide variety of ways, and (c) affiliate with new groups and adopt new roles. But we pay a price for this added flexibility: our identities are much more vulnerable than those of our ancestors. Their group would forsake them only if they became a liability. Relationships today are far more fragile. Some, such as membership in a high school or college class, are inherently temporary. Others disappear when interests or circumstances change, new opportunities arise, skills become outmoded, ideas become outdated, or people get bored and want to try something new.[58]

Are these changes life-threatening? No. But we often react as if they are because our minds are conditioned to think of identity as single, static, and, therefore, irreplaceable. So we blow threats out of proportion. We lose sight of the fact that they challenge only one component of a multi-faceted identity, and that this piece of the puzzle usually can be replaced by another that is just as good as the original.

The following scenarios illustrate how narrow, defensive mindsets develop and keep people apart.

THREAT TO A GROUP (ORGANIZATION)

Mr. Reliable

Ten years ago, Jim founded Reliable Contractors, a building repair and maintenance company that services shopping malls and office parks. Jim's younger brother, Edward, has worked as his office manager for six years, ever since graduating from college.

Nine months ago, when a severe recession hit, most of Reliable's clients began deferring all but the most essential repair work. Reliable was too saddled with fixed costs and long-term debt to make ends meet. Edward urged Jim to seek protection from creditors by filing for bankruptcy and seeking to reorganize under Chapter 11.

Jim's response: "Failure is not an option." Edward's reply: "Leaving is an option. I've got a family to feed, and I'm not going down with a ship that's sinking because the captain is too proud to save it."

When he ran out of money to make payroll, Jim was forced to close up shop. The brothers have not spoken to each other for months.

THREAT TO AN IDEA

Chained to a Plan

After Amanda became the director of marketing for a local supermarket chain last year, she set her sights on boosting sales through an aggressive television campaign featuring local celebrities. Promising a return on investment of at least 10 percent, Amanda convinced Charles, the CEO, to double the advertising budget. When first quarter sales were up only 1 percent, Amanda explained to the chief financial officer, Susan, that new ad campaigns often don't produce results overnight. When second quarter sales were flat, Susan strongly suggested that Amanda "rethink her strategy." Amanda said her strategy was great; execution was the problem. She abruptly fired the advertising firm and brought a new firm in on the spot. When third quarter sales dipped 1.5 percent, Amanda insisted the new firm needed more time to turn things around. Fearing disaster, Susan gave Charles an ultimatum: either Amanda goes or she goes. Charles promptly asked Amanda for her resignation.

THREAT TO A PERSON

A Long Shot

When Jerri was recruited as head coach of the Baltimore Harbors, she used the team's No. 1 slot in the first round draft on Ellen Tuckman, a six-foot-three-inch high school student from Indiana, rather than on several outstanding college prospects. Knowing Ellen needed a great deal of guidance both on and off the court, Jerri invited Ellen to live with her family.

A few months later, Rebecca, the assistant coach, complained to Jerri that Ellen lacked passion, discipline, and court savvy and should be benched. Furious, Jerri called Rebecca "a traitor." Rebecca resigned and the dispirited Harbors fell to last place.

THREAT TO A PROPERTY

Holding Out

The Air Force paid Vetware, a small veteran-owned firm, a fixed price of $740,000 to develop software for tracking classified documents. Jacob, the owner, and his staff of three worked nights and weekends for months to meet the Air Force's specifications. Vetware retained rights to the software.

Dent Industries, a major defense contractor, expressed interest in purchasing the tracking software for resale to other military clients. Jacob demanded $20 million—the amount reportedly paid by another large defense firm, Leland-Jones, two years ago for an encryption program. Dent's representative, Loren, offered $5 million, contending the software "had some useful innovations" but was "not unique" and "still had some bugs." Furious, Jacob said anything less than $15 million would be an insult. Loren made a "final offer" of $8 million. Furious, Jacob told Loren she "had no idea what she was talking about," and she was "just trying to screw a small businessman."

Dent developed its own tracking software, which became the industry standard. Vetware's rights became worthless.

Each of the above stories involves a proposed exchange that fails because one party equates his or her self-worth with an organization, idea, person, or piece of property and uses a single, narrow yardstick to gauge success.

In "Mr. Reliable,"

- Edward offers to continue working for Reliable Contractors if Jim agrees to protect the company from insolvency.

- Jim rejects Edward's demand as unreasonable because he equates bankruptcy with personal failure.

In "Chained to a Plan,"

- Susan (implicitly) offers to continue supporting Amanda's tenure with the company if Amanda agrees to cancel the celebrity advertising campaign.

- Amanda rejects Susan's offer because she equates her self-esteem not with the health of the company but with the success of her advertising concept.

In "A Long Shot,"

- Rebecca (implicitly) offers to continue serving as assistant coach if Jerri agrees to bench an ineffective player.

- Jerri rejects Rebecca's offer because she has hitched her self-image to Ellen's success on the court.

In "Holding Out,"

- Loren offers to purchase software from Jacob for $8 million.

- Jacob rejects Loren's offer as unfair because he equates his self-worth with the software's value and needs at least $15 million to feel successful.

Losing perspective and fixating on a single, static view of identity is most common when someone either devotes a significant portion of their resources (e.g., time, effort, or money) to achieving a goal,[59] or publicly commits to achieving an outcome.[60] But it also happens when far less is at stake. What is abundantly clear is that everyone falls into this primitive mind-set from time to time.

Disputes frequently "take on a life of their own" because one or both parties lock into a single, static notion of "winning" and hitch their identity to this idea. A minor spat about household responsibilities turns into a vicious struggle over "who's boss." A disagreement about the terms of an insurance policy evolves into prolonged litigation. An argument about the terms of a trade pact blossoms into bloody warfare.

BEST PRACTICES FOR NARROW, FIXED VIEWS

1. Maintain a Broad Perspective

When a conflict arises, ask the person in the mirror the following questions:

- What does this dispute say about me?

- What would it mean if I was wrong?

- What would it mean if I did not get my way?

- How I am determining what a fair outcome would be?

- To whom am I comparing myself?

- Would other comparisons be valid?

- How do people I respect view this dispute?

- How would they react if I adopted a different point of view, changed strategies, or altered my demands?

If "must," "cannot," "have to," or similar absolutes crop up in your answers, try to step back and gain a broader perspective. Think as broadly as possible about what interests are at stake and what options would allow people you respect to regard you positively.

2. Help Others Regain Perspective

Going negative: When someone stubbornly clings to a view you dis-agree with, the natural reaction is to let them know how frustrated you are with their stupid, pigheaded attitude. Occasionally this works: if the other party respects you, harsh words may serve as a wake-up call. Far more often, however, this competitive strategy backfires. Focused on defending a fixed position, the other party regards criticism as a threat. The greater the threat, the more angry and defensive the reaction. (See Chapter 6, page 118.)

Recall that one of the ways the unconscious mind defends against at-tacks on identity is by lowering its opinion of the attacker. Tell someone you regard them as an idiot and they will start regarding you as one.

In "Mr. Reliable" (page 43), Edward's resignation did not shock Jim into reconsidering bankruptcy. Just the opposite: Jim regarded Edward as a trai-tor and stopped speaking to him. In "Holding Out" (page 44), when Loren refused to pay more than $8 million for Vetware's tracking software, Jacob did not reconsider the price; rather, he reduced his opinion of Loren's in-telligence and motives.

When disputants view each other more negatively, they see less value in cooperating. So before going negative, carefully consider whether attacks on the other side's logic and reasoning—regardless of how well justified they may seem—are going to take you where you want to go.

Framing positively: When the other side rejects a seemingly fair ex-change, reframe the situation. Note aspects of their identity or measures of fairness they are not considering.[61]

In "Mr. Reliable," Edward could have said to Jim:

> You started this company from scratch and, for the past decade, have been a huge success. You've provided customers with high-quality work, been a steady provider for your family, and been a source of solid jobs for employees. I would hate to see all that go down the drain. Reorganization seems like the most promising way to honor your commitment to everyone who counts on you.

Many other first-rate businessmen have traveled this road. Remember Sean McAvoy? He used a reorganization to save his family's business after the government suddenly canceled a major contract. Sid Gleason did the same thing—and look where he is now.

Jim's thinking is narrow and rigid: bankruptcy = personal failure. Edward encourages him to think in terms of his roles as a husband, parent, employer, and service provider. Then Edward provides a positive basis of comparison: businessmen who went through bankruptcy and emerged admired and respected.

In "A Long Shot" (page 44), Rebecca could have accentuated the positive instead of complaining to Jerri:

> I have always admired your commitment to players on and off the court. I know how much you care about them not just as athletes, but as people. I've seen you put their needs above yours many times.
>
> I think Ellen's trying to tell us that she's not ready for professional athletics. I think she's afraid to say this to your face because she knows you put your reputation on the line when you drafted her, and you've worked so hard to develop her talents. So Ellen is communicating instead by not trying hard in practice or in games. I think the best thing you could do for Ellen, and the rest of the team, is to let her out of her contract. It would probably come as a welcome relief for all.

By tapping into aspects of Jerri's identity other than her ability to produce superstars, Rebecca provides a positive framework for letting Ellen go. She transforms it from an admission of failure into an expression of commitment and compassion. If Rebecca knew of any respected coaches who had let a player go under similar circumstances, she could have strengthened her case with an analogy between their situation and Jerri's.

In "Chained to a Plan" (page 43), Susan could have relayed experiences to Amanda in which bright, highly determined people like herself used information learned from failures to achieve great success. This framework would have helped Amanda see abandoning the campaign as a positive step—a pathway to achievement—rather than an admission of failure. And in "Holding Out" (page 44), Loren could have established a favorable comparison by citing instances in which software developers received less than $8 million for similar products. She also could have called Jacob's attention to situations in which a software developer used proceeds from the sale of one product to build a robust company capable of developing even bigger and better programs.

Reframing is difficult. Your message may take a long time to sink in, and massive doses of restraint, empathy, creativity, and patience may be required to overcome the resistance you encounter. But the payoff can be huge. The magic moment when mental blinders finally swing open and the light of truth shines through ushers in a profound sense of relief. What had previously seemed both absolutely essential and severely threatened

now seems debatable and dispensable. From this new vantage point, a protracted stalemate can finally come to a close.[62]

Challenge #2: Hoarding Information

Our minds evolved to address conflicts between members of a small community in which everyone operated from the same limited body of knowledge. Today, a common reason why people disagree about what is fair is that they operate from very different sets of facts. Communication that could bridge this gap often does not occur. Why? Knowledge is power. Yielding power to another party helps if they use it to reach a fair agreement but hurts if they exploit it to their advantage.[63]

The risks associated with disclosing information can be managed but never eliminated, so they must be taken into account. Nevertheless, the potential benefits deserve equal weight. This is where our self-serving bias creates problems. Our minds unconsciously inflate the value of our information (because it is ours) and deflate the value of the other side's information (because it is theirs).[64] So we think the other side is demanding more power (value) than they are willing to provide in return, and we refuse to trade (communicate). The opportunity to reach a favorable agreement is lost.*

Best Practices for Revealing Information

1. Disclose in Increments
Lead off by sharing information of little value, or a small quantity of high-value information. If the other side reciprocates—discloses information of equal or greater value—confidence in their good intentions should grow. Build momentum by slowly sharing more information, or more valuable information. Keep following this pattern as long as the other side reciprocates. Every exchange should increase trust.[65]

---

* Another factor that can inhibit communication is anxiety. When people feel threatened they perceive only two possible responses: fighting (competing to win) and fleeing (avoiding a confrontation). Sharing information does not further either of these strategies. This topic is covered in more depth in Chapter 6 (page 116).

2. Disclose to a Third Party

Disclose sensitive information in confidence to a trusted third party ("neutral"), such as a mediator or an ombudsman.[66] Armed with this knowledge, the neutral may be able to identify a zone of possible agreement the parties cannot see. As negotiations progress, the neutral may request permission to disclose some confidential information in order to seal a deal. At this point, the balance may tip in favor of disclosure because the potential benefit (a good deal) is readily apparent, and fear that the other side will misuse the information to its sole advantage has faded.*

A MIXED PACKAGE

NextDay's core business is delivering parcels overnight from one business to another within a large metropolitan area. It charges a high premium to deliver to addresses outside main business districts.

Door2Door provides a two- to three-day delivery service within the same metropolitan area for much lower, uniform rates.

Relationships between the companies are tense. Door2Door sued NextDay three years ago for false advertising and trademark infringement. NextDay filed a bid protest six months ago after the city government awarded a contract to Door2Door. Both suits are pending.

The number of professionals working from home, at least part-time, is rapidly increasing. NextDay's president, Roman, wants to claim this potentially lucrative market before national competitors muscle him out of the way. So does Samuel, the president of Door2Door.

Both Roman and Samuel think their best hope lies in a merger or alliance, but they hesitate to contact each other for three reasons. First, they do not want to give the other party the upper hand in negotiations by seeming too anxious to make a deal. Second, to have an in-depth discussion, they will have to share

---

* A third strategy is to sign a nondisclosure agreement (NDA), which is a promise by both sides to use shared information solely for the purposes of reaching agreement. NDAs suffer from two limitations. First, a party may be able to exploit shared information to its advantage in negotiations. Second, NDAs are often hard to enforce because determining what happens to information after it leaves your hands is difficult.

confidential market research and data about their operations. Both fear the other side may terminate negotiations and use this information to siphon away customers. Third, their lawyers have advised them to avoid contact with each other, to avoid revealing information that could be exploited in litigation.

Roman and Samuel cannot eliminate the risks associated with disclosure, but they can reduce them by disclosing incrementally, through a third party, or both.

Incremental Approach: Roman expresses interest to Samuel in "getting together to see whether we can reduce some of the friction between our companies." If Samuel responds favorably to this vague overture, Roman can become increasingly specific about his aims. Should Samuel continue to react positively, Roman can gently steer the conversation toward the work-at-home market and gauge Samuel's reaction. Roman and Samuel could then discuss how a merger or alliance might work by using a single neighborhood or type of customer as an example. Only data regarding this neighborhood or market segment would have to be shared at this point. Roman and Samuel would not have to reveal the bulk of their business-sensitive information until they felt the prospects for a profitable relationship were good.

Third Party Intervention: Roman asks his attorney to try to settle the pending litigation through mediation. In a caucus, Roman reveals his interest in a merger or alliance and asks the mediator to float this concept to Samuel as her own idea.

Challenge #3: Lack of Respect

Since traditional societies were small, stable, and homogenous, they could establish clear norms for engaging in common activities—including the airing of disputes. In a vast, dynamic, and diverse community, developing and maintaining shared practices is far more difficult. Thus, in the 21st century, notions of what constitutes appropriate behavior can vary widely. Conflicts arise whenever we fail to live up to each other's expectations, even if these slights are inadvertent.

Another key driver of conflict is the pace at which we live. Even when expectations are clear, competing priorities often take precedence. People know they should take the time to communicate face-to-face, listen carefully, and answer questions patiently. But they whip out a brief text message instead, or dash out the door when more needs to be said.

When people feel disrespected, they attempt to right the balance any way they can. Respect is a form of social value; however, as we have seen, one form of value can be converted into another.[67] If someone treats you unfairly, you can attempt to even the score by seeking material value (e.g., money) or proclaiming that they violated your rights. For example, what motivates many suits for medical malpractice is poor communication.[68] A patient or surviving relative perceives a physician as rude, curt, or aloof, or regards hospital staff as uncaring and unhelpful. A judge cannot order a physician to answer questions more thoroughly or develop a warmer bedside manner. So people sue for money instead.[69]

"Webscan" (page 37) demonstrates what can happen when someone is inadvertently treated in a way they regard as disrespectful. In that scenario, Amanda unconsciously perceived the following exchange:

- She would provide the executive committee with a marketing plan and presentation (information/material value).

- The executive committee would furnish either (a) a coveted assignment, or (b) appreciation for her efforts and feedback on why she was not selected.

The assignment would have entailed both a bonus (material value) and higher status (social value). Appreciation would have conveyed social value. Feedback would have provided material value (information).

Why did Amanda sue? Because Transnat did not live up to its side of this implicit bargain. It neither put her in charge of Webscan nor thanked her for competing and let her know why she lost. Having failed to receive the social and material value to which she felt entitled, Amanda attempted to even the score by suing Transnat for sex discrimination.

BEST PRACTICES FOR SHOWING RESPECT

1. Identify Status Concerns

Regardless of what anyone says a dispute is about, consider whether—and to what extent—it is actually driven by perceptions of unfair treatment. When someone demands material value or vindication, consider whether they want it for its own sake or its symbolic value. When people incur costs as a result of having been treated unfairly, they need money to pay bills. But money often serves partly, if not entirely, as a symbol of respect. People want it not to spend it, but to demonstrate that they have a right to be treated well by others.[70]

2. Address Status Concerns

If a dispute is fully or partially about unfair treatment, tackling these concerns head on will produce the best results at the lowest cost.

Effectiveness: If what someone truly wants is social value, what will satisfy them most is social value, not a consolation prize. To a malpractice victim who yearns for an apology, extra cash is a poor substitute. To an employee who wants notice and feedback, a finding of discrimination years later is a hollow victory.

Cost: Litigation over rights is expensive. Material wealth is zero-sum: the more you give, the less you have. Social value is infinitely expandable. Treating one employee respectfully does not diminish your ability to treat others equally well. Loving one child unconditionally does not deplete the amount of love you can shower on other children. Gestures of appreciation, concern, respect, and other forms of social value are the best deal in town: highly prized by the recipient; cost-free to the provider.

Imagine if, in "Webscan," the parties agreed to mediate immediately after Amanda filed suit. To demonstrate his concern, Steven, the chief marketing officer, attended in person and listened intently as Amanda explained how hurt and abused she felt when no one bothered to notify her that Ravi had been selected or explain why he was chosen. Steven apologized, explained why Ravi was selected, and suggested ways Amanda could position herself for the next choice assignment.

CHOOSING A MEDIATOR

Three "styles" of mediation have emerged:

Evaluative: Disputes are about rights. The mediator assesses the strengths and weaknesses of the parties' positions so they can craft a settlement that reflects the likely outcome at trial.

Facilitative: Disputes are about material value. The mediator helps parties craft a settlement that addresses their interests with regard to money, property, and information.

Transformative: Disputes are about social value. The mediator helps the parties recognize each other's thoughts and feelings as legitimate and empowers them to communicate effectively.

Top mediators refuse to be corralled into a single approach. They shift seamlessly from one to another as a discussion unfolds. Why? Disputants may be interested in all three types of value: material, social, and rights. In a commercial case, discussion may center for hours on money and then suddenly branch off into concerns about dignity and respect. A family mediation may center on relationships issues until the very end, when one party raises serious concerns about money. So the best style is going with the flow.

Amanda still feels entitled to money both to pay legal bills and to punish Transnat for neglecting her until she filed suit. But having received so much social value through mediation, Amanda no longer needs a court victory or a huge settlement to feel vindicated.

From Transnat's standpoint, the return on investment is excellent. In just a few hours, Steven resolves costly and embarrassing litigation and restores a relationship with a valued employee.

Mediation is the modern-day equivalent of ancient rituals for resolving disputes. In traditional societies, respected elders served as peacemakers. Elder statesmen play the same role today. Their wisdom provides an accepted gauge of fairness. Their imprimatur validates the result.

Challenge #4: Callous Behavior and Futile Responses

Our ancestors had no one-time, casual relationships. They interacted with the same small cast of characters repeatedly. This is why their emotions were geared for reciprocity. If someone treated them unfairly, they had to make the wrongdoer pay. Otherwise, they would be ripe for exploitation again and again.[71]

But today we frequently encounter situations in which it is either impractical or impossible to right a wrong because the perpetrator is unknown or out of reach. A driver nearly dents someone's car pulling out of a parking space, then drives off without leaving a note. A teenager anonymously posts hurtful comments in an Internet chat room just for the fun of it.

Even if you know who treated you unfairly, there may be no means at your disposal to even the score. In a civilized society, the state holds a monopoly on the power to punish.[72] Only the police may arrest, only government attorneys may prosecute, only duly appointed judges and juries may convict, and only authorized penal officers may carry out sentences. Through civil laws, the government regulates nearly every facet of life from parking, zoning, and construction to immigration, health care, and bandwidth. If you think your insurance company unjustly denied a claim, you can pursue an appeals process. But you cannot shoot the person who denied the claim in the head. By outlawing vigilante justice, civilized societies have greatly reduced rates of violence.[73] The price of peace is restraint: we must suppress our thirst for revenge.[74]

Situations in which people feel they can act with impunity—do wrong without being punished—trigger callous behavior. As Lord Acton put it, "Power tends to corrupt, and absolute power corrupts absolutely."[75] Remove the threat of retribution and revenge, and selfish impulses can run rampant. Some people always feel compelled to treat others fairly, even if they wear a crown or occupy a corner office.* But others lose their inhibitions. They are the ones who don't leave notes when they should, and who make disparaging remarks when they should not.

Best Practices When Someone Treats You Unfairly

1. Confrontation
Whenever possible, communicate about differences in person, not remotely. People generally feel more accountable when they interact face-to-face. The telephone, e-mail, and social networking sites create emotional distance. You can hurt someone's feelings without experiencing the suffering first hand.

2. Restraint
When you feel someone has treated you (or someone you feel obligated to protect) unfairly, ask yourself three questions:

1. Do you or the person you want to protect have an ongoing relationship with the wrongdoer?

2. Is punishing the wrongdoer likely to prevent future harm to you or someone you care about?

---

* Many people believe reciprocity applies in all situations, so they never feel free to treat others unkindly. This is the case if you believe God observes and judges every action; or that whatever goes around eventually comes around in some way, shape, or form—either in this lifetime or the next one.

3. Are the benefits of exacting punishment likely to exceed the costs?

HERE! IT'S NOT NEARLY AS SWEET, BUT IT'S MUCH HEALTHIER.

If the answer to one or more of these three questions is "no," then the best practices are very simple: (1) let go, and (2) move on. This advice is as easy to give as it is difficult to follow. The emotions that propel us to right wrongs are extremely powerful because of the fundamental role they play—or once played—in governing relationships. Suppressing the urge for retribution or revenge is extremely dissatisfying. But, in the 21st century, it is often the best course of action.

The first two stories that follow describe situations in which pursuing a wrongdoer makes sense. The second two are examples of where it is best to let go and move on.

U NO BETR

A neighbor tells Phil that his seventeen-year-old daughter, Annabelle, was driving erratically while texting. When Phil confronts Annabelle, she makes up a lame excuse ("I was super late . . . . I had to let my boyfriend know . . . if I'd pulled over I would've been even later!"). So Phil takes Annabelle's car keys away for a full month. As a result, Phil has to chauffeur a very surly teenager to and from school, extracurricular activities, and social engagements.

In return for providing Annabelle with a car, Phil expects her to operate it safely. When she fails to hold up her end of the bargain, he reclaims the car. Was this conflict worthwhile? Yes. Phil has an ongoing relationship with Annabelle, and taking the keys away is likely to change her behavior. The hassle of chauffeuring Annabelle around for a month is well worth the benefit of preventing a serious accident.*

WATCH OUT

Ontime sued Discounts, Inc. for repeatedly stocking and selling multifunction watches made in China, in violation of Ontime's patent. Discounts offered to settle for $100,000—Ontime's estimated lost profits—but balked at signing a consent decree that provided for ongoing monitoring of its watch sales and stiff penalties for future violations.

Ontime's CEO spent $1 million to try the case in order to send a strong message to Discount and other retailers that it would not tolerate patent violations. Ontime estimated that if "cheap knockoffs" became widespread, they could cost the company millions in sales each year.

---

* If Annabelle causes an accident, the government will step in and punish her. But unless and until a tragedy occurs, Phil remains responsible for disciplining his daughter.

Viewed as an isolated event, spending $1 million to recover one-tenth that amount seems foolish. But Ontime's CEO is gambling that, in the long-term, the deterrence value of punishing the wrongdoer will far exceed the upfront investment.

FIRED UP

When a guest inadvertently tips over a candle, the country inn Marta owns and operates incurs fire, smoke, and water damage in the dining and sitting rooms. She is forced to cancel reservations for three months while repairs are made. Marta promptly files a claim with Comprehensive Insurance for $89,000. The adjuster is slow to respond, challenges every aspect of the claim, and keeps requesting additional substantiation of losses. Finally, the adjustor offers $38,000. Marta is outraged.

Her attorney, Marilyn, tells Marta that Comprehensive is notorious for making stingy offers and playing hardball in court. After making a few phone calls, Marilyn says she can get the adjuster up to $55,000 and strongly advises Marta to take it. Fuming, Marta says she "cannot let Comprehensive get away with this." Years of expensive and agonizing litigation ensue.

In exchange for premiums, Marta expects Comprehensive to process claims in accordance with the policy. When Comprehensive appears to be cheating, Marta pushes back even though the fight is fruitless. Marta does not need to maintain a relationship with Comprehensive; she can switch carriers. And her suit is unlikely to deter Comprehensive from low-balling other policyholders in the future. If Marta had accepted the $55,000, let go of her claim for more, and moved on to rebuilding her business, she would have been much better off.

DELAYED REACTION

The child custody agreement for Samantha, age four, and Troy, age six, states that their father, Louis, will pick them up for a weekend visit every other Friday evening at 5:30 p.m. Helen, their mother, never has the children ready on time. She routinely keeps Louis waiting at least fifteen minutes. Louis is firmly convinced that Helen is being vindictive. He thinks she enjoys using any leverage she has to make him miserable.

Even though Louis is incensed, he never protests. Louis does not want Samantha and Troy to experience any more strife. He also does not want to give Helen the satisfaction of seeing him upset; he figures this will only heighten her desire to keep him waiting. Instead, he sits in the car and reads a book or catches up on phone calls. After a few weeks, the children begin to complain about having to wait inside while their daddy is out front. Helen relents.

Does Louis have an ongoing relationship with Helen? Yes, and it is destined to last at least until Samantha turns eighteen, fourteen years from now. Is Helen treating him unfairly? Yes, she is not complying with their agreement. Does Louis feel like exacting revenge? Absolutely. But Louis recognizes that, for his children's sake, he needs to suppress this emotion. No good would come from giving into it.

INTUITION

It's not what a man don't know that makes him a fool, but
what he does know that ain't so.

—Josh Billings

Intuition compares the present to the past in order to guess the future.
These guesses come packaged as emotions.

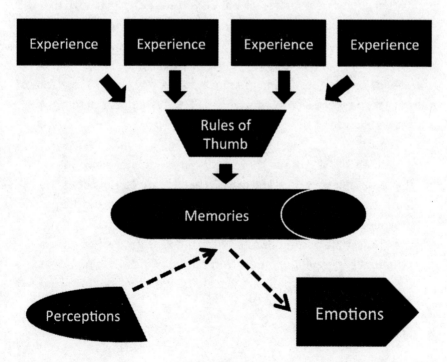

Intuition operates 24/7, instantly reacting to whatever the mind perceives. We can neither turn it off nor control how it operates.[76] But our conscious minds can chose not to act on intuition, just as they can override other types of emotions.[77]

FORMING MEMORIES

Memories include both facts (what happened) and emotions (feelings about what happened). Two key rules of thumb (heuristics) aid in forming facts and feelings into patterns that help predict the future.

Rule # 1: Events Are Caused by What Precedes Them

Memories are worthless unless formed into chains of causation. If you broke your leg last week and want to avoid breaking it again, just remembering that you broke your leg will not do you any good. You need to recall what caused the break so you can avoid making the same mistake twice.

Determining causation with scientific accuracy requires painstaking research, testing, and retesting. People rarely have the time, skill, or resources for such rigorous analysis. Instead we rely on a simple rule of thumb: a result is caused by what precedes it. If A happens before B, then A presumably caused B.

When Jill, a curious three-year-old, sticks her hand into a flame, what lesson does she learn? That fire burns. How does she learn this? By assuming that if A (getting close to the flame) precedes B (sharp pain), then A caused B.

This simple assumption (rule of thumb) allows Jill to form a potentially lifesaving memory without knowing anything about the physics of flammable materials or biological reactions to intense heat.

Rule #2: The More Often a Pattern Repeats Itself, the More Reliable It Is

If B follows A once, then the next time A happens, we have a hunch B might follow. If B follows A one thousand times, we fully expect that the next time A happens, B will follow.[78]

Being very curious, Jill wonders whether her experience with the flame was just a fluke. So she sticks her hand out again. Ouch! And a third time...yipes! Jill is now convinced that fire always burns.

THREE IS A CHARM

A common children's game illustrates how strongly this rule influences decision-making:

Child: "What do you do at a mall?"
Adult: "Shop."
Child: "What do you clean floors with?"
Adult: "A mop."
Child: "What's the opposite of 'bottom'?"
Adult: "Top."
Child: "What do you do at a green light?"
Adult: "Stop."

The correct answer, of course, is "Go." Nevertheless, bright and well-educated adults who "know" better often will answer just the opposite. Why? As Lewis Carroll put it, "I have said it thrice: What I tell you three times is true."[79] When the mind detects a pattern (e.g., the answer will end in "op"), it assumes the pattern will continue even though there is no logical reason to believe this is the case. Logic is a tool of the conscious mind; it has no bearing on intuition.[80]

APPLYING MEMORIES

Since the present is never a carbon copy of the past, intuition always involves guesswork. The unconscious mind can never be sure whether memories from the past will accurately predict how a new situation is going to unfold. To help it guess as reliably as possible, the unconscious applies the following rules:

Rule #3: Use the Most Reliable Information

Experience teaches which factors most accurately predict how a person, organization, object, or idea will behave. We also learn from experience what information has little or no predictive value. Thus, the unconscious mind focuses on the most reliable predicators and disregards other information.[81]

While visiting an amusement park, Jill slips away from her mother, Merrill, and wanders off through the crowd. When Merrill realizes Jill is missing, she immediately scans the crowd for a police officer. How? By focusing on what past experience has demonstrated to be the fastest and most accurate predictor of who is and who is not a police officer—a blue uniform.

Best does not mean perfect. Merrill may overlook an undercover or off-duty officer, or she may mistake a maintenance worker or sailor for a cop. But no factor other than a blue uniform will identify a police officer more quickly or accurately.*

Rule #4: Rely on the Most Comparable Experience

The best predictor is whichever past experience most closely resembles present circumstances.[82] Nearly identical experiences are best, but if

---

* This is why police wear uniforms and why the uniforms have become highly standardized. We want police officers to be easily recognizable.

none are available, then roughly comparable experiences provide a better guide than highly dissimilar events.

When Merrill scans the crowd she notices two figures wearing blue uniforms. The first appears to be an adult male, nearly six feet tall; the second a toddler only two feet tall. Although Merrill does not recognize either person, she has met many police officers who look quite similar to the first figure but none who resemble the second. So she runs to the first for help.

Rule #5: Rely on the Most Recent Experience

The more recently an event occurred, the more likely it is to occur again. The longer a memory lingers without being repeated, the less likely it is to recur. So, unless they are reinforced by recent events, memories fade (traumatic events are an exception).[83]

When Officer Hughes joined the police force twenty years ago, children were most strongly attracted to animals, particularly large ones. In recent years, however, video screens (particularly large ones) have become the main draw. So when Merrill tells him about Jill, Officer Hughes's gut tells him to check the entrance to the arcade first. There Jill is, transfixed by a giant screen displaying animated figures.

FORMING OPINIONS

The unconscious mind uses at least four types of predictors to form opinions about people, property, and ideas.[84]

Attributes are features that can be seen, heard, felt, or otherwise detected with our senses.

Possible sources of information about people include

- looks (size, shape, skin color, etc.)

- dress (clothing, jewelry, hairstyle, etc.)

- tone of voice and accent

- mannerisms (hand gestures, posture, gait, etc.)

The unconscious taps memories of people who look, dress, talk, and walk similarly to predict how someone will behave.

The unconscious taps memories of properties (objects) that look similar and/or behave similarly.

Since ideas lack physical features, the unconscious compares other characteristics, such as subject matter and complexity.

Context is the circumstances in which someone or something is encountered.

- **Location:** What past experience have you had with people, property, or ideas you encountered in the same or a similar venue? If you meet someone in a biker bar, you may form a very different first impression than if you meet them in a university lecture hall. Similarly, your gut reaction to an idea about the existence of extraterrestrial life may be very different if you read about it in *Science* or *Nature* than if you see it in a *National Enquirer* headline.

- **What is occurring:** If you walk past a house on a beautiful sunny day when children are happily playing in the yard, you will form a very different impression than if you first encounter it on a dark, cold night when the wind is howling.

- **How others are reacting:** What do others think of the person, property, or idea that has just been brought to your attention? Are they applauding, laughing, moaning, frightened, bored, or paying no attention? What does your past experience tell you about how reliable their reactions are?[85]

Imagine Vicki is listening to a political debate on television while a "worm" (a real-time response measure of opinions from a sample of undecided voters) appears at the bottom of the screen. Even though Vicki's conscious mind regards the worm as a silly gimmick, it may unconsciously influence both her opinion about who won the debate and her decision about who to vote for.[86]

Background describes where and how someone or something originated and what it has done, or had done to it, in the past. Potentially influential characteristics about people's background include:

- ethnicity

- religion

- family

- education

- profession

- place of birth and upbringing

Relevant past experience about property may include facts about

- how it was created

- who created it

- how much it cost to create

- how it has performed

DISTRUSTING TRUSTEES

A Stanford University experiment in the 1980s illustrates how intuition works. Undergraduates were asked to critique two proposals for how the university could use its financial leverage to pressure the South African government to end apartheid (segregation and suppression of blacks). Randomly selected students received brochures describing the advantages and disadvantages of "specific disinvestment" and "deadline" plans. All brochures contained identical factual information, but some said the university supported one plan, some said it supported the other, and some said nothing about the university's position.

When told the university supported the deadline plan, 85 percent of students thought the other plan (specific disinvestment) represented a greater concession by the university. In contrast, when told the university favored specific disinvestment, only 40 percent of students thought this plan was a larger concession.[87]

Why were so many students influenced by the university's alleged position? Few, if any, knew enough about university finances to consciously analyze the plans. They had to rely on intuition instead. What would be an accurate predictor? Many students firmly believed the trustees were more interested in protecting the university's bottom line than they were in helping oppressed South Africans. So when told the trustees favored the "specific disinvestment" plan, the students felt the other plan represented more of a concession. When told the trustees favored the "deadline" plan, the students felt "specific disinvestment" imposed a greater burden.

Intuition uses what it knows to guess at what it does not know. When presented with an idea outside our realm of expertise, the most relevant knowledge we may hold is memories about the person (or board) who is advancing the idea. So we form an opinion about the idea based on these memories.

- what others have paid or offered to pay for it

Pertinent background information about ideas may include:

- how it was created

- who created it

- what circumstances lead to its creation

- what motivations lead to its creation

Character is defined by how someone or something behaves. Aspects of people's character include their

- temperament

- reliability

- attitude

- thoughtfulness

- values

Property is characterized by different features:

- quality

- durability

- dependability

- economic value

FORMING OPINIONS ABOUT ORGANIZATIONS

Intuition about groups and organizations is based on the people, property, and ideas associated with them. A company may be embodied by a founder or chief executive, a sales representative, a manager or employee at a local retail outlet, or a celebrity spokesperson. The property associated with an organization may be a distant but well-known site (e.g., the Pentagon or the Sears Tower) or a local factory, office, or store. Ideas may include a company motto, mission, or methodology.

INTUITION AND CONFLICT

Most intuitive guesses are correct, and some are brilliant. By identifying and honing in on one or more highly accurate predictors, the unconscious mind may instantly, effortlessly leap to a better conclusion than the conscious mind can deliver after weeks of rigorous deliberation. But it may also be dead wrong. And intuition has clever ways of concealing its mistakes.

When people make snap judgments others regard as misguided and unfair, conflicts arise. We look first at what causes intuitive errors and then examine why these errors, once made, are difficult to recognize and correct.

Types of Intuitive Errors

Intuitive mistakes can result from one or a combination of the following problems.

MISPERCEPTIONS

People sometimes think they see, hear, touch, taste, or feel something that is not actually there. Misperceptions lead people to form faulty memories of the past or misconstrue the present.

When her neighbors, Roberto and Mercedes, passed by yesterday, Andrea was shocked to see Roberto yelling and gesticulating madly while Mercedes cried in silence. This morning, Andrea saw Mercedes talking animatedly while Robert stared off into the distance with a smug, self-satisfied expression on his face. Andrea got a strong vibe that their marriage was on the rocks.

Andrea is completely off base. She failed to notice that her neighbors were using their new Bluetooth headsets. Yesterday, Roberto was yelling at his sister, Rosalita, for having been rude to Mercedes at a family reunion the day before. This morning Mercedes was speaking with Rosalita, who had called to apologize. Mercedes was very moved by how forcefully Roberto had stood up for her. Their marriage has never been stronger.

MISINFORMATION

Senses supply first-hand information. Conversations, newspapers, radio, television, the Internet, and other media supply second- and third-hand information about the world. When these sources are inaccurate, people form distorted memories or develop a warped view of the present.

Mark worked as a financial consultant for a large Wall Street firm. Consistently rosy projections of future profits and growth from the CEO and other top officials gave Mark the impression that his job was secure and large bonuses were on the horizon. So Mark and his wife joined the real estate boom by signing a contract to purchase an expensive new home. When Mark awoke to news reports that his firm was bankrupt and had been taken over by the government, he was in shock.

Mark's sense of how the future was going to unfold was based on false information. Thus, his gut led him astray.

Natalie suffers a broken leg, whiplash, and bruised ribs when her car is rear-ended with enough force to set off the air bags. Anxious to gain a client, Natalie's brother-in-law, Steven, tells her she's got a "million dollar case." He includes this figure in the complaint he files against the other driver, and Steven and Natalie regularly refer to their "million dollar case" in conversations with friends and other family members.

When the defendant's insurance company offers to settle for $120,000, Natalie is incensed. The lowest counteroffer she consents to is $800,000, and she is willing to go this low only because Steven offers to cut his fee. After the insurance adjuster deems this figure "wildly unrealistic," settlement negotiations grind to a halt. After a trial that costs Natalie $20,000 (mostly for expert witness fees), the jury awards $30,000 for medical expenses and $60,000 for pain and suffering.

Natalie's sense of her case's worth was based on misinformation from Steve. Because both she and Steve repeated this figure over and over again, it became deeply ingrained in Natalie's mind as fact. The claim became a million dollar case. Just as the unconscious mind develops firm pictures of people as friendly, reliable, or cutthroat, and expects them to behave accordingly, it forms fixed views about characteristics of property such as economic value.

MISINTERPRETATION

When unrelated events follow each other in close proximity, the unconscious mind may confuse coincidence with causation. In other words, it may conclude that B followed A because A caused B when the relationship between the two was mere happenstance. When A recurs, the unconscious predicts B will follow, even though there is no reason to expect this pattern to repeat itself.[88]

Crystal manages a team of advertising executives. She assigns Raoul to create a print ad for the new Summit hiking boot and tasks Joachim with developing a Web ad for a new running shoe, the Intrepid.

Summit sales start out strong but fade rapidly in the wake of customer complaints about shoddy workmanship. In contrast, sales for the Intrepid remain flat for months and then skyrocket after a Kenyan relay team wearing Intrepids breaks a world record.

Intrepid's manufacturer wants to capitalize on this success with a high-priced, multimedia campaign. Raoul angles hard for the account, pointing to the quality of his past work. However, Crystal feels more comfortable keeping the account under Joachim.

Before their efforts were overtaken by events, Raoul's ad appeared to perform well, whereas Joachim's did not. So why did Crystal prefer to retain Joachim on what had become a high-profile account? She confused coincidence with causation. Since the Intrepid campaign succeeded under

Joachim, Crystal's gut tells her not to change horses in midstream—especially not when the other horse's ad campaign flopped. Is this rational? Absolutely not. Raoul is blameless for Summit's failure, and Joachim deserves no credit for Intrepid's success. But the unconscious mind operates by association, not reason. Joachim's drafting (event A) preceded Intrepid's success (event B), so Crystal's unconscious mind presumes that if A occurs again, B will follow.

Over 2,400 years ago, the Greek playwright Sophocles observed that "None love the messenger who brings bad news."[89] They are no more loved today because intuition still holds them responsible. Intent on forming useful (predictive) memories, the unconscious mind assigns a cause to every event based on timing. So if you happen to be around when bad things happen, or become known, other people will associate you with these unwanted events regardless of your degree of fault.

Crystal could ignore her intuition and assign the Intrepid account to Raoul, but we are strongly inclined to follow our gut even when we recognize it is irrational.

MISMATCHES

When present circumstances and past experiences are highly similar in many respects, distinctions between them nevertheless may lead to very different outcomes. If the unconscious mind misses these distinctions and views the two situations as comparable, its gut reaction will be incorrect.[90] Mismatches (overgeneralizations) between present circumstances and past experience occur most frequently when people have (a) limited information about present circumstances or (b) limited past experience with similar situations.

However, mismatches can occur even when the present looks nearly identical to a past situation. A seemingly insignificant distinction may have a large impact.

Chester is a popular and respected supervisor of a team of research biologists and support staff at the Satton Corporation. He is outgoing and friendly. As many people in the company know, Chester is deeply involved in the lives of his school-age children and church.

Chester is also obsessed with Caroline, a single mother on his team who is shy and does not make friends easily. Not only has Chester made bold advances toward Caroline at work, he has also tracked her down and pursued her during off hours.

Fearing no one will believe her, Caroline keeps talking herself out of filing a complaint. Her inaction emboldens Chester to stalk her even more aggressively. When Caroline reaches the limits of endurance and charges sexual harassment, detailing a long list of lurid behavior, everyone at Satton is incredulous. Caroline is not describing the Chester they know. Certain that a good man like Chester couldn't possibly have done what Caroline alleged, Chester's supervisor conducts a perfunctory investigation, then brings Chester back to work supervising a different team. Caroline's co-workers vilify and ostracize her for what she said about Chester.

Chester continues working at the Satton Corporation until a jury convicts him of stalking and a judge sentences him to prison.

Once we feel we know someone's character, we feel we can predict their behavior in any context. However, many "brave" people are extremely fearful in certain situations (e.g. public speaking); many "brilliant" people are inept in some subjects; and many "good" people, like Chester, have a serious moral failing or two. The unconscious mind presumes a level of consistency few of us live up to.[91] Thus, Chester's colleagues were thoroughly convinced of his innocence; whereas a jury with no preconceived notions found Chester guilty beyond a reasonable doubt.

Derrick and Lilly are in the midst of a bitter divorce in which both have framed "who gets the house" as the touchstone of "victory." This is partly because they both love the house and partly because their ten- and twelve-year-old children love it too.

After consulting a therapist, Lilly suggests a compromise: She and Derrick co-own the house and reside there when they have custody (and elsewhere when they do not). The children (and dog) stay put. Neither Derrick nor Lilly need a second home large enough for the children—a major cost savings.

Derrick rejects the idea out of hand. He can't point to anything specific that he dislikes; it just reminds him of all of the other screwed up, impractical "Lilly" schemes he stupidly went along with and later regretted.

Instead of considering the merits of Lilly's proposal, Derrick categorically rejects it based on his experience with other ideas she has advanced.[92] As a result, he sabotages what might be the best plan for everyone involved.

Even if Derrick's recollection is accurate (which is unlikely),[93] that does not necessarily mean Lilly's current idea is unsound. None of us are either right or wrong all of the time. Once it detects a pattern, however, intuition overlooks evidence that an exception may apply (such as the fact that Lilly developed the idea with professional advice).

Why Intuitive Errors Are Difficult to Recognize and Correct

Once someone makes an incorrect decision based on a gut reaction, two factors may prevent them from recognizing and correcting the error. The first is that some intuitive errors become self-fulfilling prophecies by generating evidence that appears to confirm their validity. The second is self-promotion: our unconscious tendency to interpret information self-servingly. (See Chapter 3, page 29).

HOW INTUITION REINFORCES ITSELF

When people make decisions based on gut reactions, their actions alter what they experience. These experiences inform their intuition; their intuition, in turn, influences future decisions.

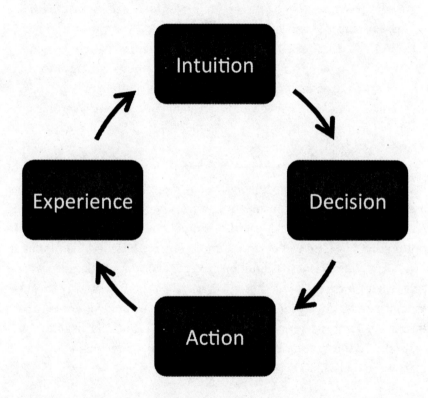

Here is an example of how this feedback loop works.

THE BRIEF ENCOUNTER

Fresh out of law school, Sam and Veronica secure entry level positions in the procurement law section of a state agency. Elizabeth, the chief counsel, has a backlog of routine matters and one high-profile case on which she needs immediate support. When she first lays eyes on the new hires, her gut tells her Sam is better equipped to jump into the high profile case, so Veronica gets stuck working through the backlog.

The high-profile case affords Elizabeth an opportunity to mentor Sam on research and writing and to observe him perform under pressure. Having no time left over for Veronica, Elizabeth assigns an already overloaded staff attorney to mentor her.

Since Elizabeth has developed confidence in Sam, while Veronica remains an unknown quantity, Elizabeth feels far more comfortable assigning sensitive and complex matters to him.[94] So Sam receives progressively more challenging work while Veronica falls further behind.

Elizabeth's initial gut reaction, and the decision she makes in light of it, provides Sam with opportunities to showcase and improve his skills that are denied to Veronica. Since Sam performs well, Elizabeth assumes the pattern will continue. Lacking information about Veronica, Elizabeth cannot predict how she will perform, and therefore Elizabeth continues to favor Sam. Was Elizabeth's intuition correct? Did Sam's initial success and subsequent progress prove her gut was right? There is no way to know. Veronica never got to compete with Sam on an even field. But Elizabeth interprets Sam's performance as proof positive that her intuition was accurate. So the next time Elizabeth makes a personnel decision, she will place even more faith in her snap judgments.[95]

HOW SELF-PROMOTION REINFORCES INTUITION

When Elizabeth favors Sam with choice assignments and superior mentoring, his performance becomes an extension of her identity. If he becomes a star performer, she basks in his glory. If Sam screws up and Veronica becomes the star, Elizabeth looks foolish. So Elizabeth promotes her identity by unconsciously interpreting Sam's performance favorably and Veronica's unfavorably.[96]

21ˢᵀ CENTURY CHALLENGES

Relying on intuition in a fast-paced, complex world creates a wide variety of problems. But we have to make the best of the mental tools at our disposal.

Challenge #1: Increased Dependence on Intuition

This is the so-called Information Age. The quantity of knowledge created in recent decades far exceeds all of the learning generated in the thousands of years of human history that preceded them. And thanks to the Internet, we can access much of this knowledge with a level of ease and speed our forbearers could not possibly have imagined.

So has intuition's primitive method of forming opinions gone the way of the horse and buggy? Have we finally lost our need for its simple rules of thumb? Paradoxically, the knowledge revolution has rendered us more dependent on intuition, not less. Why? The more there is to know, the more each person knows about less and less. As our range of expertise narrows, we must lean on intuition to guide us through an ever greater range of activities.

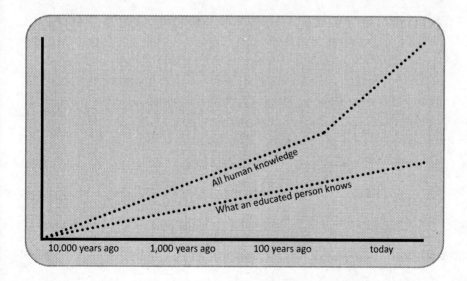

When people first began transmitting knowledge through writing, they knew precisely how their writing instruments worked because they crafted them with their own hands. When pens, paper, and ink became available for purchase, writers could easily judge the quality of these materials by examining them. Today, most information is transmitted via electronic devices whose inner workings are an utter mystery to most users. So people decide which device to purchase intuitively, typically using one of these predictors:*

- Recommendations from friends or experts. If Gwen's or Harry's previous recommendations about technology have been useful, their future recommendations are also likely to be useful.

- Past experience with a particular manufacturer. If previous CompuPac devices have worked well, a new CompuPac device is also likely to work well.

Leveraging what you know to guess at what you do not know is not a sophisticated or precise means of reaching decisions. Most of the time, however, it is the best any of us can do.

Challenge #2: Intuition Has Become Less Reliable

Modern life has undermined our capacity to intuit accurately in a number of ways. This section explores three developments: the ability to control our environment, the ability to communicate remotely (without face to face contact), and our ever-increasing tendency to disregard what is happening right in front of our eyes because of distractions.

---

* Reason will get you part of the way. You can use it to determine whether you want a laptop or a desktop, how much memory you need, and how much you can afford to pay. But unless your technical knowledge is highly advanced, it will not tell you which computer in your price range is the best value.

CHOICE

Unable to shape their environment, hunter-gatherers took life as it came. So although their experience—and consequently, their intuition—was very limited, it accurately reflected the world they inhabited. By exercising control over our lives, we shape memories. They reflect the choices we make about lifestyle (firsthand experience) and education and entertainment (secondhand experience). Residents of rural farming communities, gated suburban enclaves, and struggling inner cities have sharply different experiences with people, property, and ideas.

People who get their news from MSNBC, Fox News, Al-Jazeera, or a neo-Nazi website form highly contrasting memories of how the world works.[97]

If airplane crashes and shark attacks, although extremely infrequent, receive extensive coverage whereas drunk driving fatalities and teenage suicides, which are far more common, receive scant attention, our sense of danger (an aspect of intuition) becomes skewed. Our gut tells us to avoid activities that are relatively safe and pay insufficient attention to serious risks.[98] Most people know (consciously) that the vast majority of Muslims are peaceful and law abiding. And this conscious knowledge accords with their firsthand experiences. But secondhand sources are dominated by stories of extremist violence. The constant repetition of ghastly images leaves us with the gut sense that Muslims are more threatening than other people.

In addition to choosing what we want to learn about the real world, we also choose what fantasies to experience. The conscious mind clearly understands the difference between fact and make-believe because imagination is central to decision making (see Chapter 5, page 101). But intuition operates solely on experience. In nature, everything is real so there was no reason for the unconscious mind to learn how to segregate fact from fiction. This is why we enjoy stories; they excite our emotions even though we know (consciously) they are untrue. But while we are entertaining ourselves, our unconscious mind is developing a sense of how real people, property, and ideas behave based in part on memories of events that never actually took place. Every choice you make about what novel to read, television sitcom to watch, or movie to view shapes your intuition in ways you cannot observe or control.

REMOTE COMMUNICATION

Unable to read or write, hunter-gatherers always communicated face to face. They did not need to verbalize their emotions; visual and vocal cues (facial expressions, gestures, tone, timber, and inflection) conveyed their feelings. Our minds are innately adept at interpreting these cues.[99] No one has to teach a baby to cry when it is hungry or uncomfortable, and no one has to teach mothers that babies cry to signal unmet needs. We know intuitively whether someone looks or sounds happy or sad, content or frustrated, pleased or angry, proud or envious.[100] But an ever-increasing amount of communication occurs remotely. The telephone conveys vocal cues but no visual information (unless video conferencing is available). E-mails, text messages, blogs, postings, and other writings offer no clues about emotion unless the author chooses to include them (e.g., "I am angry" or, better yet, "I AM ANGRY!!"). And words rarely, if ever, convey emotion with the depth and richness of a knowing wink, a wry smile, an angry growl, or a soothing hum.

Imagine Morgan texts Jonah a party invitation and he texts back, "Sure, that would be great." To determine how to react, Morgan must infer Jonah's intent and decide which of the following he means:

- I am genuinely excited.

- I am pissed off and being sarcastic.

- I am not excited but am willing to make the best of it.

- Sounds good unless a better offer comes up.

Since intuition operates 24/7 based on whatever information is available, no matter how limited,[101] Morgan will develop a sense of Jonah's subtext. But her margin for error is large. Had she invited Jonah in person and witnessed his reaction, Morgan would be far more likely to gauge his reaction accurately.

Because so much interaction is now both remote and instant, misunderstandings arise and get escalated at the drop of a hat. Gary misunderstands Gabrielle's intent and fires off an angry reply. Gabrielle is infuriated by Gary's inappropriate reaction and fires off an even more venomous response. The sparks fly.

CROSS-CULTURAL COMMUNICATION

Another 21st century challenge is misunderstandings that occur when people from different cultures try to communicate. All people, regardless of upbringing, are naturally inclined to express emotions the same way. But layered on top of our natural inclinations are cultural norms about how emotions should be expressed or suppressed.[102] In many cultures, for example, boys are taught not to express sadness by crying. Girls are often taught to smile and seem agreeable even when they feel otherwise.

So if you are unfamiliar with someone's culture, you may misconstrue the emotional signals they are trying to send. You may interpret a nod as a "yes" when it really means "not yet," or think someone is avoiding eye contact to be rude when their true intent is to show respect. The more diverse our communities become, the harder we must work to understand each other, even when we communicate in person.

INATTENTION

Even if someone is standing just inches away, you will miss key emotional cues if your attention is elsewhere.[103] The faster life comes at us, the more distracted we are by competing priorities. Many misunderstandings occur simply because people fail to notice what is readily apparent.[104]

Challenge #3: Intuition Is More Suspect

As society has become more dynamic and diverse, informal customs and traditions have given way to formally adopted rules (laws, regulations, bylaws, etc.). To comply with formalities, we must furnish reasons for decisions in situations such as these:

- To impose discipline without running afoul of a collective bargaining agreement or a corporate personnel manual, a manager must explain why an employee deserves to be punished in a particular manner.

- To defend against a claim of malpractice, a physician must articulate how his decisions fell within accepted standards of practice.

- When appearing before a grievance panel, a professor must provide reasons why a student's final paper merited no more than a C+.

Since people often make decisions based on their judgment (intuition), when challenged they are forced to invent reasons.[105] Since intuition is based on factors we not aware of, these reasons often inaccurately portray the basis for a decision.[106] Nevertheless, the strength of these made-up excuses becomes the crux of the dispute.

BEST PRACTICES FOR USING INTUITION

The best way to prevent and avoid disputes is by making decisions others regard as fair and reasonable. Since intuition is error prone, but we cannot get by without it, how do you decide how to decide? There are several factors to consider.

Time. If you need to make an instantaneous decision, go with your gut. Intuition works a lot faster than reason.[107]

Quantity of information. Intuition works best at the extremes. If you know too little to make a reasoned decision, intuition's rules of thumb provide a good guess.

CONVENTIONAL WISDOM

Flashes of brilliance that seemingly appear out of nowhere inspire unbridled faith in intuition. They also fuel popular myths about a sixth sense or extra-sensory perception (ESP).

Snap judgments that lead to calamity demonstrate the compelling importance of casting feelings aside and waiting patiently for all the facts to arrive.

Thus, popular advice about intuition is completely contradictory:

"Go with your gut."   "Don't judge a book by its cover."

"Follow your heart."   "Don't let your heart rule your head."

"Trust your instincts."   "Don't jump to conclusions."

"Avoid the paralysis of analysis."   "Keep an open mind."

"If it feels good, do it."   "Think before you act."

Consequently, it is completely useless.

If you must sort through a huge quantity of data, intuition also may be your best guide. Since our system of education exalts reason above all else, relying on intuition to resolve highly complex problems may seem downright counterintuitive.[108] But the conscious mind can process only a limited number of variables: seven tends to be about the maximum number.[109] When faced with a mass of information, it gets overwhelmed. This is why big problems are regarded as mind-boggling and why people get confused by the facts.

The conscious mind tends to cope by oversimplifying: it hones in on the information it is most adept at analyzing and gives short shrift to the remaining data. Intuition also oversimplifies by relying on one or a small number of predictors, rather than a rigorous analysis of all the relevant facts. But these predictors have been verified by experience, so they are likely to be more accurate than the ones the conscious mind deems most relevant.

To steer your intuition in the right direction, you first need to gather and familiarize yourself with the relevant information. That requires some thought. Then step away and sleep on it (relax and direct your attention elsewhere).[110] Your unconscious mind will take over, and when you revisit the problem, you will have a feeling about what to do.[111]

Imagine Chandler is trying to determine whether his consulting company should merge with a competitor. There are at least four issues he should consider:

- whether they will achieve economies of scale and become more efficient, or become more bureaucratic and less efficient

- whether combining personnel will create synergies or trigger in-fighting and backstabbing

- whether current clients will think the merged organization provides better service or is less attentive to their needs

- whether prospective customers will be more or less likely to sign up.

Under each factor are numerous sub-issues. Chandler could stay up all night devising a matrix for critiquing all the available information with regard to each factor and sub-issue, and then for giving proper weight to each factor and sub-issue relative to the others. But he will fare at least as well, if not better, by having a relaxing evening and a good night's sleep and seeing how he feels in the morning.

Skill. Are some people intuitive and others analytical? No. These are overgeneralizations. The ability to intuit or reason well varies tremendously by subject matter. It depends on innate ability, experience, and education.[112] An investment banker may have a fabulous gift for sizing up which technology company startups will succeed but be utterly incapable of discerning how to comfort his infant daughter when she starts to wail. A trial lawyer who has a "sixth sense" of which jurors will sympathize with her client may be completely stymied whenever her computer, car, or dishwasher acts up.

If, with respect to a particular area, you are strong on book learning and weak on experience, then reason is your strong suit. If the reverse is true, intuition is your better guide. If you are unsure whether to rely on reason or go with your gut, bear in mind that we are prone to have greater faith in our intuition than is warranted. (See "Why Intuitive Errors Are Difficult to Recognize and Correct," page 78).

Imagine Irene is the director of admissions for a prestigious business school. She believes she has fabulous intuition because most of the students she selects enjoy successful careers and many reach senior leadership positions. But the students she rejected—based on her gut —may be equally accomplished. Irene has no way of knowing. So, like the rest of us, Irene needs a dose of humility.

Quality of experience. Before relying on intuition, it is critical to ask whether your first- and secondhand experiences with people, property, and ideas have furnished you with accurate memories.

1. In experiences with **people**, we are highly prone to misinterpret events and thereby form inaccurate patterns of causation. For example, consider the achievement gap between Caucasians and African Americans with respect to professions such as law, medicine, and accounting. Our conscious minds know the gap results from historical factors—slavery and segregation—and not from differences in innate ability. As creatures of experience, however, our unconscious minds learn a different lesson. Racism is an abstract concept. You cannot see it in action. What you can observe is people with dark skin achieving lower levels of socioeconomic status than people with light skin. So the unconscious mind regards skin color as an accurate predictor of professional success. Since repetition equals reliability, the more often we see white doctors, lawyers, and accountants—either in person or in movies or television shows—and black drug dealers and gang members, the more firmly entrenched our patterns become.

In short, when events are shaped by forces that are not immediately apparent, a yawning gap may develop between what the conscious mind knows and what the unconscious mind presumes. Only new experiences can narrow the divide. If you are thinking, "Not true! My brain could not possibly harbor prejudiced thoughts!," then sample a few of the Implicit Association Tests at https://implicit.harvard.edu/implicit. They reveal unconsciously held beliefs by measuring how long it takes to select the "socially correct" (unbiased) answer. Since gut reactions are instant but conscious deliberation takes time, slow but unbiased answers indicate unconscious bias. For example, if it takes longer to associate "trustworthy" with "Jewish" than with "Christian," or to associate "manager" with "woman" than with "man," then the test taker harbors unconscious bias against Jews and women. Knowing exactly how the test works will not affect your score because intuition lies beyond conscious control.

Results from the Implicit Association Tests include the following:

- 48 percent of African Americans show a pro-white or anti–African American bias.

- 36 percent of Arab Muslims manifest an anti-Muslim bias.

- 38 percent of gays and lesbians hold negative attitudes toward homosexuals.[113]

Why are so many people unconsciously biased against their own group? Because, like everyone else, they experience discrimination first-hand and read and watch biased reporting from secondhand sources.

RESHAPING INTUITION

A Yale University study conducted in 1997–1998 showed that male U.S. congressmen with daughters voted more in line with positions approved by the National Organization for Women (NOW) on twenty issues than those without daughters. The tendency was even stronger among congressmen with more than one daughter. The "daughter effect" transcended party affiliation; both Democratic and Republican fathers were impacted.[114]

For the purposes of this analysis, the point is not that aligning more closely with NOW is either "good" or "bad." It is simply that novel experiences reshape intuition in ways we cannot control and are often unaware of. So if you want to try to change your intuition, experience something new. But recognize that rules of thumb beyond your conscious reach will weave the new patterns.[115]

Human resource managers in Boston and Chicago told researchers they were aggressively pursuing minority candidates. To test how effective their efforts were, the researchers sent four resumes for the following candidates in response to 1,250 help-wanted ads in local newspapers:

- an average candidate with a "white" name (e.g., Greg or Cindy)

- an average candidate with a "black" name (e.g., Tyrone or La-Teesha)

- a highly-skilled candidate with a "white" name

- a highly-skilled candidate with a "black" name

Candidates with "white" names received 50 percent more callbacks than candidates with "black" names. In fact, average "white" candidates fared significantly better than highly skilled "black" candidates.[116]

What happened? Well-meaning human resource managers mistakenly assumed their intuition would align with their objectives. But when they saw a "black" name on a resume, they rated the candidate lower than a "white" candidate with poorer credentials. By so doing, they perpetuated the evil they had set out to reverse.

What could these well-intentioned human resource professionals have done differently? To the greatest extent possible, they should have shielded themselves from information that was irrelevant and likely to lead their intuition astray. The following examples illustrate how this might happen.

Recruiting staff. During the initial screening, ask an assistant to cover over names before you (and other reviewers) review resumes. Deprived of these potential clues to gender, race, or ethnicity, you will be better able to focus on relevant factors such as education, training, and on-the-job experience.* Many educational institutions now avoid bias through anonymous grading. Instead of writing their names on examinations or papers, students provide an identification number.

In interviewing, use a structured process:

- Prepare job-related questions in advance.

- Ask each candidate the same questions in the same order.

- Take notes on their answers.

- After all interviews are completed, compare the answers side by side.

- Reserve judgment until you have completed this entire process.[117]

Determining the questions in advance prevents you from steering the interview in a particular direction based on a snap judgment. If your gut says someone "looks right" for the job, you may be tempted to dispense with hard questions and focus on selling them on your company. In contrast, if your gut tells you someone would not be a good fit, you may be tempted to cut the interview short, thereby depriving the candidate of a chance to prove himself.[118] This is yet another example of how intuition generates self-fulfilling prophecies. A structured process counteracts this tendency.

---

* This is not a foolproof system. Entries on a resume—such as varsity football or a leadership position in a sorority—may provide ready clues to gender. Some colleges are known to be predominantly African American, Catholic, or female. Nevertheless, covering over names helps remove one source of potentially biased information.

Suspending judgment until the process is complete will help you evaluate the candidates' answers objectively (based on substance) rather than in light of how you felt about them at the time. The first time you force yourself to compare answers side by side instead of relying on your sense of which interviewee "was the best fit," you may be amazed at how far your final decision deviates from your initial gut reaction.

Reviewing and rewarding. When nominating employees for an award, training opportunity, or coveted assignment, do not list whichever names pop into your head first. Instead, develop a list of relevant traits and rate each eligible employee based on these criteria.[119] Do not be surprised if someone you initially overlooked turns out to be better qualified than the employees you thought of first.

Similarly, when conducting performance reviews, compare employees based on objective criteria instead of relying on your sense of how well they performed. This shortcut is extremely tempting for busy managers, but it can easily backfire by leading to unfair decisions that touch off protracted, time-consuming disputes.

Because customers are just as susceptible to bias as anyone else, do not assume their feedback is objective. In recent studies, female and minority employees were rated lower than white male employees who performed the same tasks in precisely the same way. Similarly, all other things being equal, groups with a high concentration of white males were rated higher than groups with more racial and gender diversity. [120]

Promoting. To avoid bias in promotions (and recruiting), many organizations now require that decisions be made by "diverse" review panels. But given that people often harbor prejudices against members of their own group,[121] diversity is not an adequate substitute for policies and procedures that promote objective decision making.

2. Snap judgments about **ideas** are frequently based on experience with the person (or group) who generated or is advancing the idea. Usually these judgments serve us well. Imagine, for example, that you are sick and your physician recommends a particular steroid. Unless you are medically trained, using your conscious mind to critique this recommendation is not an option. But intuition will tell you whether to trust this physician or obtain a second opinion.

Unfortunately, when disputes arise, people tend to distrust and devalue ideas advanced by the other side.[122] To avoid such misguided reactions, conceal the source of an idea. A neutral third party can help. In the divorce scenario on page 78 above, Lilly could have communicated her house-sharing proposal in confidence to a mediator. In a subsequent meeting with Derrick, the mediator could have raised the idea without revealing Lilly as the source. Derrick would then have had an opportunity to weigh the idea on its merits instead of dismissing it out of hand as one of Lilly's follies.

When a neutral go-between is unavailable, brainstorming can help depersonalize ideas. Participants first list all the ideas they can think of for resolving the dispute without evaluating them or indicating their source. Then, they consider the advantages and disadvantages of each idea. Third, based on this analysis, they discuss which ones they do and do not favor, and why.

Like structured interviews, brainstorming sessions reduce the influence of unreliable gut reactions by forcing participants to consider objective criteria before passing judgment. If Derrick and Lilly had taken this approach, by stage two the connection between Lilly and house sharing would have gotten weaker, and the advantages would have become apparent. So, in the end, Derrick might have to come favor the idea.

In multiparty conflicts, allow participants to provide input anonymously. More ideas will flow, and they will be evaluated more objectively.

3. Disputes about **property** commonly center on value. A prospective buyer and seller cannot agree on the price of office space, or a plaintiff and defendant cannot agree on the value of a legal claim. When it is not possible to determine value objectively—by plugging facts into a formula—disputants have no choice but to rely on their intuition. Frequently, their judgment is heavily influenced by what others think.[123] For example, most art fans would agree that the Mona Lisa is priceless, but few could say why. Their sense of value is based on the fact that the Mona Lisa is one of the best-known paintings in the world and is revered by respected art critics. Judging value based on what others think, like judging ideas based on who advances them, is effective if your sources are reliable. In conflicts, however, parties frequently distort facts to suit their interests, so their judgment is suspect.

For example, researchers asked judges to rule on a hypothetical case in which the plaintiff suffered injuries in a car accident caused by a negligent truck driver. The driver admitted liability (fault) but disputed the amount of damages. Judges in the control group received no specific information about what the plaintiff (accident victim) was seeking. Judges in the test group were told the plaintiff was unwilling to settle for less than $10 million—an unusually high number in light of the facts. The average award from the judges in the control group was $808,000. Awards from the test group judges averaged $2.21 million—significantly more than double.[124]

The amounts that plaintiffs demand and defendants offer to settle a lawsuit are notoriously unreliable indicators of value. In an effort to gain the upper hand, both sides generally throw out numbers far above or below what a judge or jury is likely to award. This is why, in real life, judges and juries are not privy to settlement offers.[125]

If you are a party to a dispute, however, and you want to try to reach an agreement, you cannot shield yourself from settlement proposals advanced by the other side. These proposals will influence your judgment about value. The only question is how much influence they will have. Studies show that each additional dollar a claiming party first demands in negotiation typically results in a 50 percent increase in the settlement amount agreed to by the other side. Even among seasoned negotiators who are (consciously) aware of the impact that an initial "anchor" can have, final settlements typically rise 37 percent for every dollar increase in the first serious settlement proposal.[126]

So how do you avoid being "anchored" by the other side into paying too much or accepting too little? By evaluating value as objectively as possible. Disputants frequently do not prepare adequately for settlement negotiations.[127] They fail to identify and analyze alternatives, assess risks, and determine transaction costs. Moreover, as is discussed in Chapter 5 (page 108), they often fail to clarify their interests and goals.

When you are involved in a dispute, the more thought you put into determining what a fair outcome would be, the less you will be influenced by what the other side says is fair.

A DELEGATE RELATIONSHIP

To demonstrate how easily our thinking about numbers is influenced by other numbers, researchers rigged a roulette wheel to stop at one of two spots: 10 or 65. After the ball landed at one of these locations, participants were asked how many African countries are members of the United Nations. Since few, if any, knew the correct answer they had to guess (rely on intuition). Among participants who saw the ball land on 10, the median response was twenty-five. Among participants who saw the ball land on 65, the median response was forty-five.[128]

Why such a significant difference? The unconscious mind never views events as random; it sees causation everywhere. So when it sees a low number, it expects this number to cause the next number to be low as well. The same goes for high figures. The participants in this study undoubtedly understood, on a conscious level, that roulette wheels do not determine membership in the United Nations. Nevertheless, their unconscious minds detected a causal relationship based on timing.

HELPING OTHERS SEE THE
ERROR OF THEIR WAYS

If you believe someone else's judgment is incorrect, resist the temptation to argue your case; instead challenge them to explain how a contrary viewpoint could be correct.[129] Arguing puts people on the defensive. They "win" (bolster their self-image) by refuting your points. In contrast, when people try to construct their own alternative viewpoint, they win by demonstrating how competently they can perform this task.[130]

PART III
THE CONSCIOUS MIND

REASON

The test of a first-rate intelligence is the ability to hold
two opposed ideas in the mind at the same time, and
still retain the ability to function.
                                    —F. Scott Fitzgerald

We use reason (rational decision making) to determine how best to
fulfill desires.[131] In other words, we think in order to figure out how
to get what we want.[132]

Step 1. The conscious mind uses its powers of imagination to generate
options based on facts culled from experience and learning.[133]

Step 2. It uses a rule (belief) or rules to analyze which option is best.
Consciously applied rules are learned, not innate (hard-wired). They
include laws, customs, and ethical principles; scientific principles; religious
precepts; social and cultural norms; the policies, practices, and procedures
of an organization; instructions from an authority figure; a formal or
informal code of conduct within a family or social group; personal experience; and the seeds of a fertile imagination. They also include many of the
same rules of thumb (heuristics) employed by the unconscious mind.[134]

Step 3. The conscious mind implements a decision. When the decision
is to suppress a strong emotion, this is the hard part. Deciding to quit

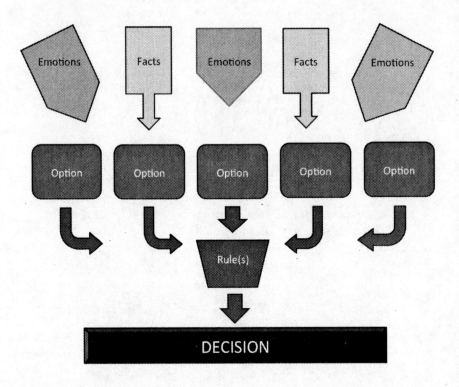

smoking or lose fifty pounds is easy; mustering the willpower to follow through can be daunting.

Decisions are hardest when

- the stakes are high; strong drives are in play.

- the situation is unclear; relevant facts are ambiguous, voluminous, and/or complex.

- numerous options are available; many choices would satisfy at least one desire.

- the options are difficult to assess; no rule applies, or multiple, conflicting rules (beliefs) apply.

In short, deciding is easy when you do not feel strongly one way or the other, when you have only one option, or when you have multiple options but one is clearly best. Deciding is most difficult when the consequences are significant and no good option exists or it is unclear which alternative is best.

THE CONSCIOUS MIND AND CONFLICT

Disputes are like icebergs: the biggest and most treacherous part often lies hidden below the surface. What you can plainly see is a disagreement between two people. What you cannot see are the conflicts raging within the minds of these individuals.

Internal conflicts may involve one (or more) of the following:

- **Competing desires regarding the same material interest.** Martin decides to fulfill his need for sustenance by dining at his favorite restaurant. The waiter describes two specials that sound fabulous. Martin must choose between the two.

- **Competing material interests.** There is a blizzard raging outside and the Fisher family has run out of food. Dad wants to go to the supermarket to buy provisions but fears for his safety.

- **Competing material and social interests.** Amy ran eight miles this morning and is starving. Karen, her manager, offers to take her out to lunch as a reward for working long hours last week. Karen picks an upscale nouvelle French restaurant with tiny portions. Amy wants to order six courses to appease her appetite, but she does not want to appear boorish or greedy.

- **Competing social interests.** Adrian has been close friends with both Sophie and Bruce since college and would like to maintain these relationships. But the couple is going through a bitter divorce, and Bruce has demanded that his "true" friends take sides—that is, stop socializing with Sophie.

- **Competing desires regarding the same social interest.** Bernice is the only female employee on a team of electrical engineers. At a recent staff meeting, a fellow employee told a sexual joke that Bernice found offensive. She wants to be regarded as a full member of a team, not the odd woman out. Bernice feels like telling everyone jokes like this make her feel excluded, but she also feels like smiling and laughing to show she is one of the guys.

A conflict between two emotions produces a third emotion: the desire to invent an option that eliminates the need to make a hard choice. So the upside of internal conflict is that it sparks creativity.

STAYING GROUNDED

Deborah, a commercial real estate agent, is running late for an important meeting with a client on the sixteenth floor of an office building. She is standing on the ground floor, nervously awaiting the arrival of an elevator. About twenty people with NorthQuest ID badges are waiting alongside her. Deborah glances at the list of tenants—NorthQuest is on the ninth floor.

When an elevator finally arrives, Deborah desperately wants to push her way on, hit "16," and go. Nevertheless, she waits politely for passengers on the elevator to exit and for people who have been waiting longer to enter. Then, out of the corner of her eye, Deborah spots a maintenance man. She explains her predicament and asks whether there is a nearby service elevator she could use to head straight up to the sixteenth floor. He says yes. Problem solved.

Facts: Deborah is running late, some NorthQuest employees have been waiting longer for an elevator than Deborah, and several elevator passengers wish to exit at the ground floor.

Emotions: Deborah wants to get to the meeting as quickly as possible. Deborah does not want to appear rude.

Initial Options: (1) get to the meeting quickly by pushing past other people; (2) wait patiently and get to the meeting later.

Applicable rules: (1) allow people to exit an elevator before entering; (2) allow people who have been waiting longer than you to enter an elevator first; (3) arrive at meetings on time.

Initial Decision: Being boorish is more antisocial than being late, so it's best to wait patiently for others to exit and enter the elevator.

New Emotion: Deborah wants to find a way to get to the meeting fast without being rude.

New Fact: There is a service elevator.

New Option: Take the service elevator.

Revised Decision: The new option is best because it allows Deborah to avoid being late without being rude.

21ˢᵀ CENTURY CHALLENGES

In one respect, we have it much easier than our ancestors. Many of their decisions had life-or-death consequences. Every time they hunted a large animal, or gathered food where predators might be lurking, they risked mortal injury. Progress has reduced the risks associated with meeting basic needs to a minimum. Decisions today are mostly about how to satisfy wants or preferences, not how to meet essential needs.

But two factors cut the other way: an ever-expanding number of choices and an ever-decreasing supply of clear rules for how to choose. Want to invest your savings? The number of available stocks, bonds, mutual funds, and money markets, both domestic and international, has increased exponentially in recent decades. Want to spend your savings? The quantity and variety of goods and services readily available for purchase has skyrocketed and keeps multiplying by leaps and bounds.[135]

Freedom of choice has blossomed because many laws and customs that constrained behavior have been overturned. People are no longer expected to move lockstep into the roles their parents and grandparents filled. Race, ethnicity, gender, religion, country of origin, and socioeconomic class may influence behavior, but they no longer dictate it. Society has become far more tolerant of alternative lifestyles. Instead of mandating conformity, it celebrates diversity.

BONES OF CONTENTION

Dateline: One hundred years ago

Shauna and Amos have an eleven-year-old dog, Phoebe, with a growth on her leg that is interfering with her gait and making her moan and cry. The veterinarian says it looks like bone cancer, which he cannot possibly cure or treat. He suggests putting Phoebe down immediately to spare the dog any further pain. Shauna and Amos exchange quick, sad glances and then ask the vet to go ahead.

Dateline: Today

The veterinarian refers Phoebe to a specialist who offers an array of possible treatments involving surgery, chemotherapy, and radiation. All would cost several thousand dollars and require numerous trips to the hospital with Phoebe and a lot of home treatment and care. The more aggressive therapies would cause considerable discomfort but might extend Phoebe's life for several weeks or months; it is hard to tell.

Old fact: cancer is incurable. Old rule: animals served people. New facts: lots of complicated options with costs and benefits that are hard to weigh. New rule: ???. Many people now treat animals as family members, making great sacrifices for their sake. How much time and effort is it appropriate to spend on a dog? How much suffering should you inflict on a dog in order to try to extend its lifespan? From a canine's standpoint, is surgery more or less intrusive than chemo?

Shauna and Amos cannot make up their minds about what to do. Pressed by the specialist for a decision, they begin arguing with each other.

BEST PRACTICES FOR REACHING AGREEMENT

Dispute resolution is usually less about brilliance than it is about willpower. Some problems cannot be solved without a burst of creativity, but the key ingredient in most situations is self-discipline.

Resolve Your Internal Conflicts First

1. Step Back
Conflict resolution must begin from within. Disengage from the other party until you clarify your own interests.

This advice is far easier to dispense than follow because people often either fail to recognize that they are internally conflicted, or they recognize the problem but do not want to deal with it. Instead they blame their frustration on someone else.

We refer to tough choices as "painful" because they literally are. Emotions demand to be fulfilled. When we fail to heed their call, they create suffering. The most intense pain generally comes at the moment of truth: when a decision is made to forego one desire for the sake of another. The limbo that proceeds this moment, when all opens remain open, can be less disquieting. So prolonging an external dispute can be a strategy for escaping internal pain. In a divorce case, for example, a party may balk at signing a settlement agreement because they do not want to acknowledge that the marriage is over. Unfortunately, postponing the day of reckoning can be very costly: legal bills keep mounting. Animosity usually does, too.

2. Clarify

We move from confusion to insight by translating feelings into words and forming words into the logical structure of sentences and paragraphs.[136] Thoughts can be verbalized orally or in writing. People often think out loud by talking to a pet, a houseplant, or the stars that shine at night, not because they are expecting a clever response but because no response is necessary. The learning comes from listening to their own musings.[137] Fleshing out thoughts in a diary, a journal, a strategic plan, or some other type of document is as good or better a way to get your arms around an internal conflict.

3. Respond

Once you understand an internal conflict, you can make a rational decision about how to proceed. If your decision is unlikely to sit well with the other side, you may gain some sympathy by explaining your internal struggle and how you resolved it.

Staying on the Write Side

Joni is an aspiring writer with a day job as an account representative for a software company. Hoping to finish a novel, she
asks her manager, Nicholas, for permission to work part-time for
six months. If Nicholas denies the request, Joni faces a difficult
choice. She could go over his head, but this would strain their relationship. Joni could pursue other jobs, but she might end up
even worse off. Finally, Joni could keep working full-time and hope
the novel eventually gets finished.

Nicholas says he needs a few days to think about it. Then he
reports to Joni: "I really struggled with this one. I've always
dreamed of being a writer myself, so I hate to stand in the way of
someone finishing a novel. I'm also concerned about losing a first-
rate employee. I hope that won't happen. But Finance is prowling
for positions to cut, and if I approve a part-time schedule, they'll
take that as proof we're overstaffed. I don't like to give in to that
type of pressure, but in the long run I think it could be worse for
both of us if I give them an excuse to eliminate your job."

By sharing his internal conflict, Nicholas lets Joni know that he appre-
ciates her predicament and would genuinely like to help. Joni still faces a
difficult choice. But knowing Nicholas respects her and values what she is
trying to accomplish makes staying put more palatable.

Help Others Identify and Address Their Internal Conflicts

Why is this your job? Because if others are unclear about what they
want, you cannot reach an agreement with them. Their problem becomes
your problem.

1. Recognize the Symptoms
When people who are internally conflicted try to resolve differences

with others, they tend to behave erratically or evasively (or both):

- telling different narratives about the same situation

- stating different interests at different times

- advancing contradictory assertions, arguments, or demands

- shifting from being inflexible ("I will not pay a penny more") to being flexible ("What is the best you can do?") and back again

- changing moods as different emotions come to the forefront

- declining to articulate specific interests or demands

- evading questions about thoughts, feelings, or concerns

Since we are inclined to think the worst of our adversaries (see Chapter 3, page 31), when others vacillate, shift, dodge, or hedge, we presume they are trying to manipulate or outfox us. But they may simply be confused or overwhelmed.

2. Provide Feedback

You cannot negotiate effectively with someone whose goals are unclear. They will either fail to agree to anything, or agree and then change their mind. So the only way you can protect your interests is to call attention to the problem and see whether the other party has the capacity and will to address it.

If you are firmly convinced the other side is intentionally trying to manipulate you, say so. Otherwise, note their lack of clarity or consistency without being critical. Then suggest a way to move forward, as in the following examples:

"You said you want to do whatever you can for Phoebe. You also said that you are not comfortable with spending a fortune on a pet, especially an older one, knowing that your parents may need help with medical expenses in a few years. It sounds as if you are feeling pulled in different directions. Would it help to discuss this?"

"When I asked about price, you responded that selling the home your parents built and lived in for fifty-four years for less than $900,000 was not an option. But you've been talking for the last several minutes about wanting to close quickly and being certain a deal won't fall through. It might help to list all the interests at stake here and see how they can best be balanced."

"It sounds as if you want to keep pushing forward full steam on the project in France, keep going full tilt back in Texas, and have my team cut expenses. Maybe we should establish a list of priorities."

Highlighting the other party's internal conflict will clarify the situation or signal that it is unlikely to get clarified anytime soon. Either way, you gain a clearer picture of prospects for an agreement.

3. Set a Deadline

If it is to your advantage to resolve a conflict quickly, imposing a deadline can force the other party to confront the pain associated with making a tough choice sooner rather than later.

Imagine Mary cannot decide between option A and option B. If it is within his power to do so, Tom can inform Mary he is withdrawing option B as of the close of business on Friday. If Mary prefers option B, she now has an incentive to choose it and confront the emotional pain of foreclosing option A. If Mary does nothing, the choice will be made for her.

Whose Turn Is It?

The wail of despair from the basinet pierces the cold night air. Matt's bleary eyes struggle to bring the numerals 2, 3, and 0 on the alarm clock into focus.

There is a bottle of formula on the dresser. But in a desperate ploy for more sleep, Matt focuses on the option that lets him off the hook for feeding his three-week-old daughter: "I can't believe Emma needs to nurse again."

Without seeming to waken, Ruth says Emma prefers a bottle at night.

Matt: "I've got to finish a brief tomorrow morning, sit in meetings all afternoon, and attend a networking dinner tonight. I've just got to get some sleep."

Ruth: "I was up nursing Emma every hour last night, and twice already tonight. I'm completely spent. My body's too exhausted to produce any more milk."

Wide awake now, and unable to withstand another plaintive screech, Matt grabs Emma and the bottle. "I thought we were going to have help in the house, something regular. What's up with that?"

Ruth whispers, "I'm still trying to figure that out. It takes time."

Matt is in no mood to whisper. "Well, meanwhile, I've figured out what I need: more sleep! Can you help me out here?"

Ruth picks up on his angry tone. "In case you've forgotten already, Matt, I have a career too, and I'm not getting any work done at all. I've got a grant proposal due at the end of the week, and I got zero done yesterday. I'm just trying to find a few hours to sit in front of the computer. I'm certainly not complaining about going out for fancy dinners. While you're doing that, I'll be changing diapers."

Matt: "I've been busting my butt so you don't have to work. What do you want from me?"

Ruth: "Nobody put a gun to your head and made you become a partner. Deal with it."

Too agitated after their argument to fall back to sleep, Matt and Ruth greet each other in the morning with sullen silence.

The tip of the iceberg is a dispute between Matt and Ruth over tending to Emma. Lurking beneath the surface are massive, treacherous internal conflicts about professional and personal goals. Until Matt and Ruth figure out what they want to do with their lives, they cannot reach agreement on how to raise Emma.

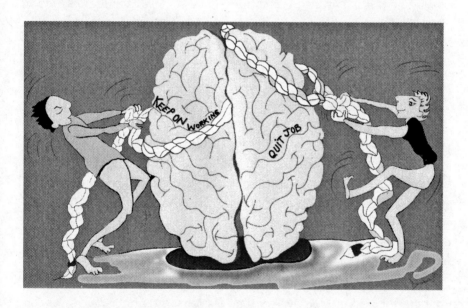

The facts. Ruth, thirty-four, is officially on maternity leave from her position as executive director of a local art museum. Competition for grants is fierce, however, so she finds herself working from home anyway. Matt, thirty-seven, just made partner at a law firm. He works an average of sixty hours per week and frequently travels for business. Ruth and Matt could afford to live on Matt's income.

The emotions. Ruth wants be a good mother, but she also cares about the world of art and wants to continue working. She feels it is important to spend a lot of time with Emma, particularly in her early years, but she also feels Emma would benefit from having a strong, independent mother as a role model.

Matt wants to provide Ruth and Emma with all the resources they need to maintain a comfortable lifestyle, just the way his father did when he was growing up. But he also wants to spend more time with Emma than his father spent with him and his sister. Matt already feels somewhat burnt out on commercial litigation, but he is very happy about the big financial payoff he is just starting to reap from many late nights and weekends at the office.

The rules. In previous generations the rules were clear: men were expected to be breadwinners, and women were expected to be homemakers. Today, at least in Ruth and Matt's social circle, there is no rule. Every couple seems to handle it differently. There are a number of stay-at-home moms and a smattering of stay-at-home dads; some moms and dads who both work full-time and split domestic chores evenly; and some couples in which one spouse works fewer hours and handles more of the child care.

The options. The primary options for Ruth are to resume full-time work when maternity leave expires, resign and become a full-time mother, or seek part-time work with less prestige and responsibility. The primary options for Matt are to stay a partner, opt for shorter hours but lower pay as "of counsel" to a firm, or make the same trade-off by securing a position as in-house counsel for a corporation. Until they decide which options to pursue, Ruth and Matt will not know whether they want full-time help or part-time help, or whether they are able to care for Emma themselves.

The analysis. Ruth is confused. She wants to be a good mother, but she is not sure what is best for Emma: a stay-at-home mom who dotes on her, or a working mom who exhibits strength and independence. If staying at home would be best for Emma but maintaining a career would make her happier, does Ruth have a right to put her needs above Emma's now that she is a mother? Ruth thought this would all become clear when Emma was born, but she remains as ambivalent as ever.

Matt is equally confused. He wants to be a good father, but he is not sure what is best for Emma. Should he be a hard-working dad who provides great material comfort but is gone a lot? Would Emma be better off with a less prosperous dad with more time to give? Matt is also not sure what he wants for himself: the prestige and creature comforts of being a partner or a less stressful job. Before Emma was born, Matt was leaning toward finding another job. Now he is less sure. His job often seems less stressful and more fun than being at home.

The decision. Matt and Ruth want to postpone the pain associated with stifling one lifestyle option for the sake of another. But delay is costly. Because they are burning the candle at both ends—pushing forward on demanding careers without help at home—they are exhausted, frustrated, and blaming each other for their problems. Their relationship is deteriorating rapidly.

Even if they were inclined to do so, Matt and Ruth cannot achieve peace through accommodation. Should Matt say, "I'll take whatever job works best for you, honey," Ruth must still decide whether she wants to work full-time, part-time, or not at all. And even if Ruth decides to stay home full-time, Matt must nevertheless decide whether he wants to keep putting in long hours at the office. The best gift they can give each other is a deadline—a quick one—for deciding how much child care they are willing and able to provide.

The price tag we pay for freedom is uncertainty. By inventing so many choices and giving ourselves so much leeway to choose, we have strained our capacity to reason.

CHAPTER SIX

ANXIETY

Raising the threat condition has . . . physical and
psychological effects on the nation.
—U.S. Department of Home-
land Security website (2005)

Only one of our three essential needs ever demands immediate attention: safety. We can last for several days without water and several
weeks without food, and we can delay bearing children for years. But
violent attacks can kill in an instant. The mind is therefore primed to
respond in the fastest possible way: through preprogrammed responses
we call instincts. No learning or choice is involved.

Immediate Danger. When attacked, we instinctively harness all of our
physical and mental energy to resist by either fighting or fleeing.[138]
When confronted with immediate danger, physical changes in the
body include:

- increased heart rate and blood pressure (to send more oxygen to
  the muscles)

- constricted veins (to send more blood to major muscle groups)

- tensed muscles (to ready limbs for action)

The brain also signals the body to prepare for traumatic injury—in case we lose the fight or flee too slowly.[139]

In the unconscious mind, anger, which motivates fighting, or fear, which motivates fleeing, reaches a peak level, and all other emotions disappear.[140]

And in the conscious mind, high-level mental functions (reason, communication, emotional control, and short-term memory) cease to function. Why? The conscious mind thinks slowly, and time is of the essence. The parts of our mind that are geared for rapid response must assume control.[141]

This is why, when people are in mortal danger, they report being "blinded by anger," "paralyzed by fear," "unable to think," "scared out of their wits," "dumbfounded," "out of control," or "so frightened they can't remember a thing."

Looming Threats. When danger lurks just around the corner, we instinctively prime ourselves to fight or flee on a moment's notice. Muscles remain tensed; eyes and ears are alert to signs of trouble. Levels of anger or fear (or both) are heightened; other emotions are only dimly felt. Emotional control is diminished. Thoughts remain focused on the source of danger. The mind rehearses, over and over again, how it will respond when the attack comes. Stuck in this singular mode, it cannot think, communicate, and remember well, nor can it relax or sleep.[142]

Dateline: 10,000 years ago. Lea is holed up on a cave, surrounded by a pack of hungry wolves. Her eyes and ears vigilantly seek any signs of movement. Her mind keeps rehearsing how she will fiercely stab the first wolf to approach her while screeching at the top of her lungs to deter the others. Adrenaline surges through her veins. She is ready to let loose with rage at any moment. Although Lea has not eaten all day, she does not feel hungry. Despite having been on her feet for hours, Lea does not feel tired. Whenever she starts to think about anything else, Lea's thoughts immediately return to the wolves.

Anxiety is a highly functional reaction to this type of threat. It helps keep Lea alive.

The greater the sense of threat, the higher the level of anxiety. A premonition of impending doom triggers extreme symptoms; vague concern prompts a mild reaction.[143]

21ST CENTURY CHALLENGES

Anxiety remains a lifesaver. The risk of suffering a sudden, violent death has greatly diminished, but it has not disappeared. People still get hit by buses or shot by intruders. But the vast majority of modern-day conflicts pose little or no risk of becoming violent. You may feel an urge to wring your surly teenager's neck or hit your boss over the head with his Blackberry, but you don't. Unfortunately, we react to verbal jibes that attack our sense of identity the same way we react to violent events that

"The areas where I see the greatest potential for growth are..."

menace our physical well-being. Our instinctive mind cannot distinguish between the two.[144]

Short-Term Consequences of Anxiety

Anxiety escalates nonviolent conflicts; it makes bad situations much worse. Most nonviolent conflicts are best resolved cooperatively: through communication, compromise, or collaboration. Anxiety primes us to respond competitively by trying to defeat or evade an enemy. The unconscious mind ratchets up the emotions that drive these competitive behaviors. The conscious mind loses the skills needed to respond cooperatively (reason, communication, emotional control, and short-term memory). Just when we most need to remain calm, cool, and collected, we blow our top.

SKETCHY INSTRUCTIONS

Angela owns and manages a commercial architecture firm. Since hiring Jim two years ago, Angela has found him to be reliable and creative.

Angela assigns Jim to draft plans for renovating a furniture store in an historic shopping district. She hands Jim a sketch drawn by the store owner, Robert Finch, and a list of Finch's requirements. She tells Jim the plans have to be completed in three weeks because Finch is on a tight schedule to open the store.

Finch, a wealthy local entrepreneur, is Angela's best customer. In addition to being a source of repeat business, Finch has referred several friends to Angela who became good clients.

Unfortunately, Finch prides himself on being a skilled designer and has no talent in this arena. Angela has kept him happy over the years through the "Finch rule": do quality work without making the client feel his input is being ignored.

Unaware of the rule, Jim begins from scratch to design a

stunning layout that draws on the best features from nearby land-marks. The day before the deadline, Jim proudly displays the draw-ings to Angela.

Angela goes ballistic. She berates Jim for ignoring instructions, wasting three weeks on useless work, and jeopardizing her rela-tionship with a key client. Shocked and incensed, Jim tells Angela she has gone off the deep end and has no clue what she is talking about. Angela orders Jim to turn over the project to her most sen-ior architect, Raul, immediately. Jim says, "Hey I can do better than that. I quit!" Furious, Angela responds. "No, you're fired! And I'll make sure you never work again."

Like all relationships, Angela and Jim's revolves around an implicit ex-change. Angela is to provide Jim with a salary and quality experience. Jim is to provide Angela with quality work. Angela perceives Jim's violation of the Finch rule as a breach of trust—and a threat to her identity as a successful business owner. So she attacks him (verbally). Jim perceives Angela's attack as grossly unfair—he thinks he lived up to his end of the bargain—so he attacks back by questioning Angela's sanity. Angela counters by reassigning the project (and, thus, implicitly attacking Jim's competence). Jim retreats into flight mode by quitting. Angela responds in kind by terminating him.

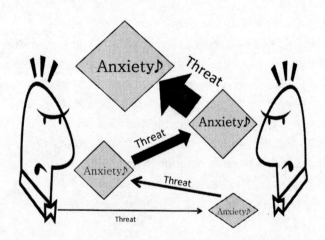

Like fire, anxiety feeds on itself, growing hotter and hotter as it consumes more fuel. Each attack and counterattack raises the level of anxiety, so the next round of attacks is even more vicious, until one or both parties decide they can no longer take the heat and flee, leaving behind the charred remains of a relationship.

For reasons covered in previous chapters, once a conflict escalates into a heated disagreement, it can become very difficult to resolve. When parties feel their identity is under siege, they are prone to develop narrow, fixed views regarding the facts of the dispute and options for resolution (see Challenge #1: Narrow, Fixed Views, page 41). Anxiety-induced repetition of these options hardens thinking even further. And because disputants regard each other as enemies, not potential partners, they see no benefit in sharing information that could lend a fresh perspective (see Challenge #2: Hoarding Information, page 51).

The conflict between Jim and Angela was ignited by a simple misunderstanding. Jim did not know about the Finch rule. Angela wrongly assumed that he did but purposely ignored it. But unless Angela and Jim seek to reconcile, or a third party steps in to mediate, they will never realize that their relationship can easily be repaired. Communication is essential for cooperation.

Long-Term Consequences of Anxiety

Mortal threats last for seconds, minutes, or hours, so our minds and bodies are conditioned to remain anxious only for short periods of time. Modern, nonviolent conflicts can linger for days, weeks, months, or years, especially if they find their way into the legal system. The prolonged anxiety triggered by these disputes can have devastating physical and mental effects. The risk of damage to blood vessels, the heart, and kidneys increases significantly,[145] as does the risk of developing a viral infection, cancer, diabetes, and digestive disorders.[146] Sleeplessness impairs our ability to function, and its effects are cumulative.[147] The more nights in a row of fitful sleep, the worse our concentration. To cope with anxiety, people often engage in unhealthy habits such as smoking, drinking, and overeating.[148]

When people say they are sick and tired of conflict they mean it —often even more literally than they recognize. Anxiety-induced fatigue has an upside: it may ultimately bring parties back together. But not until they are utterly worn out.

BEST PRACTICES TO REDUCE ANXIETY

Since anxiety is an automatic response to threat, the only way to reduce someone's level of anxiety is to help them feel less threatened.[149]

Timing

When an argument gets heated, you must **disengage** quickly—before anxiety strips away the self-control you need to do so. Like much of the advice in this book, this is far easier to suggest than to follow. When we do not want to concede that an adversary has the power to upset us, we deny feeling threatened (e.g., "I am NOT angry!!") When we do not want to concede that an adversary has the right to feel upset, we tell them they are overreacting and need to calm down. In other words, a competitive mindset leads us to fight about what ought to be happening instead of responding to what is happening—a dangerous escalation—until it is too late to shift gears.

Reengage and reestablish communication as soon as possible after calm has been restored. The longer a dispute lingers, the more deeply entrenched the parties become in their outlook. Furthermore, because anxiety is so wearing on both body and mind, delay can truly be unhealthy.

Location

Select an environment you and the other party perceive as nonthreatening. What spot is best for discussing a conflict is highly contextual. A familiar environment is sometimes best because it feels secure. An unfamiliar, neutral location is sometimes best because it has no negative history. A private setting may feel comfortable because it is quiet and confidential. A public setting may feel safer because it puts pressure on the parties to maintain decorum, and help is immediately available if someone loses control.

While there are generally distinct advantages to meeting face-to-face (See Chapter 3, page 59, and Chapter 4, page 84), if both parties would prefer to communicate via phone, e-mail, or instant messaging, do not rule out these options. There is no universal right way to reduce anxiety; what matters is how the parties perceive the options available to them.

Format

Establish guidelines. One or both parties may be concerned about the discussion getting heated, particularly if this has happened before. You can calm fears by proposing a code of conduct. Guidelines can be formal (written and precise) or informal (oral and general). They can also be positive (prescribing behavior) or negative (proscribing behavior). Agreeing to listen to what the other party has to say and to treat each other respectfully are positive guidelines. Promising not to curse, interrupt, or make sarcastic comments are negative guidelines. A combination of both may be appropriate.

If you suspect a discussion may become hostile, propose guidelines before the sparks start to fly. Asking "Can we agree not to interrupt each other?" at the outset sounds neutral. But asking the same question after the other party has interrupted three times sounds critical and, consequently, may fan the flames.

Guidelines are a dramatically underused way of reducing anxiety. They need not be elaborate. Before engaging with a teenage child about his late-night habits, you can ask, "Can we agree to listen to what each other has to say with an open mind?" Even a teenager can recognize that it is hard to say no to such a request without seeming foolish. And this one, simple rule may lay the groundwork for a useful discussion.

Include other Participants. Another way to reduce anxiety is by including people who can help keep the discussion on an even keel. A neutral third party is the most obvious choice. Mediators and facilitators model appropriate behavior for the parties. By remaining calm, optimistic, and lighthearted in the midst of conflict, they subtly encourage the parties to do the same.

Party representatives, if wisely chosen, can also help bring peace into the room. While some lawyers are naturally combative, many do an excellent job of keeping clients in check. Friends and family members can also play a supportive role.

Preparation

Writing out thoughts not only aids in identifying and sorting out emotions (see Chapter 5, page 108), it also helps control them. When nervous students spend a few minutes before a big test jotting down their fears and concerns they feel calmer—and they perform better.[150] Writing down in advance what you feel anxious about may help you remain more relaxed and focused while discussing a contentious dispute.

Content

When the other party's anxiety seems disproportionate to the threat, look for ways to alter their perception. As we saw in Chapter 3 (page 48), reframing can be the key to regaining a healthy perspective on a conflict.

In some situations, what the other party most fears is an action you are not planning to take. If this is the case, let them know up front. They may become far less anxious. Similarly, if what you most fear may or may not come to pass, it may be appropriate to ask the other party at the outset what their intentions are. You may find you have less to fear than you imagined.

PART IV
PUTTING IT TOGETHER

CHAPTER SEVEN

CHANGE

Even smart people are really pretty incapable of
envisioning a situation that's substantially different
from what they're in.

—Christine Peterson, Vice-President,
Foresight Nanotech Institute

This chapter combines lessons from prior chapters to address two key 21st century challenges: transitioning quickly from one emotionally charged experience to another, and anticipating how you will feel in circumstances you have not yet experienced.

TRANSITIONING

An emotion, once triggered, lingers until one of the following events occur:

• Words or actions satisfy the urge.

• In reaction to a dramatic development, the unconscious mind produces a more powerful emotion.

• In reaction to gradual changes, the unconscious mind produces an array of other feelings.

In other words, emotions last until they are expressed (acted upon), suddenly pushed aside by a more urgent call, or slowly crowded out by other feelings. Thus, after a triggering event ends, a strong emotion may survive for a long time before other feelings finally push it aside. Steadfast feelings are commonly referred to as moods.

Anger and fear are our most powerful emotions, so they have the most staying power. Anger fuels aggressiveness and fear fuels caution, so our bad moods often push us in one of these directions. But good moods can be dangerous too. Exuberance stokes optimism, which can inspire unwise risks.

Transitioning to a new activity while in a distinctly good or bad mood creates two closely related problems. First, decisions are likely to be driven by emotions unrelated to the situation at hand.[151] Second, since the mind is clouded by strong feelings, it may fail to pick up on important emotional signals from others. The stronger your emotions are, the less capable you are of empathizing with others (unless their feelings are the same as yours).[152]

Thanks to technologies that permit instant communication anytime, from virtually anywhere, people now constantly shift their attention from one subject to another. If you do not respond to e-mails during a meeting, toggle between two telephone or instant messaging conversations at once, or work on one project while teleconferencing about another, you surely know others who do. Most of these interactions are routine. But the few that set us off create an emotional danger zone.

Best Practices for Transitioning

When you feel strong emotions. When an event triggers strong feelings—positive or negative—step off the multitasking bandwagon long enough to regain equilibrium. Time saved through making better decisions will far exceed time spent composing yourself.[153]

Finding a positive outlet for emotions is the fastest way to get back on track. Unburden yourself to a friend, go to the gym, meditate, write, hop on a bike—whatever suits your personality. Withdrawing from the world until your mood changes also works, although not as quickly.

If you must transition immediately from one emotionally charged encounter to another, notice what feelings you carry over and try to factor them out of your decision making. The more cognizant you are of which events triggered which emotions, the better equipped you will be to make fair decisions.[154]

When you need support from someone else. Before raising a potentially controversial subject, take a few moments to assess the other person's mood, particularly if you are communicating remotely and do not know what is happening at the other end. A few brief questions such as "How are you?" "How is your day going so far?" "Did you just get out of a meeting?" "Are you in the middle of something?" or "Did I catch you at a good time?" may provide important clues. If the answers concern you, find a delicate way to delay the conversation. In our hypercharged world, people often feel pressured to respond immediately to every request. Let them know very clearly that you are willing to wait.

If you have no reason to suspect someone's mood might be off until they respond inappropriately, circle back as delicately as possible. As the following examples illustrate, there are ways to highlight the problem without putting the other person on the defensive:

- I was not expecting such a strong reaction. Are there factors at work here I might not be aware of?

- That is not the reaction I was expecting. Did something happen recently that might have changed your point of view?

When someone recognizes they let a bad mood influence a decision, they may apologize and reverse course.

Collision Course

Peter pulls into the company parking lot after being stuck in traffic for two hours because of a three-car pileup on the freeway. He is fit to be tied.

Good transition: Peter nods a quick hello to a few colleagues, shuts the door to his office, and quietly works his way through routine administrative work for forty-five minutes. By the time he reemerges for a meeting, Peter's spirits have lifted.

Lucky transition: Before Peter can get out of the car, Scott hugs him, reports that the company just landed a huge contract that will double profits, and hands Peter a bottle of champagne. Peter is trilled. Traffic woes suddenly seem like ancient history.

Bad transition: Furious about being so far behind schedule, Peter immediately summons Eric for a briefing that was supposed to have started an hour ago. When Eric indicates progress on a key project is even slower than expected, Peter tells him in an uncharacteristically threatening tone that he had better turn it around quickly—or else. Eric cannot believe his ears.

Note: To prevent this blowup, Eric could have prefaced his remarks by asking Peter how his morning was going so far, thereby affording Peter an opening to vent about the traffic before hearing unwelcome news.

Down on Reserves

Kacie, who chairs the board of a nonprofit organization, discovers at a routine examination that she has a lump in her breast that needs to be biopsied. While walking out of the doctor's office, Kacie receives a call from her executive director, Charlene.

Good transition: Kacie tells Charlene she just received some potentially bad news and is not in a frame of mind to be talking about business right now. Kacie directs Charlene to consult with the chairs of the board's finance and special project committees and promises to check in with her in a week or two.

Bad transition: Kacie listens while Charlene requests permission to finance a potentially lucrative but risky fundraising initiative out of the organization's reserves. After quizzing Charlene about various ways this venture could go wrong, Kacie tells Charlene this is just not the right time for a big risk. Charlene is stunned.

Note: Charlene should have begun the conversation by asking Kacie whether this was a good time to discuss a new initiative. Alternatively, she could have requested an in-person meeting instead of catching Kacie off guard with a bet-the-farm idea.

ANTICIPATING

Humans are not adept at predicting in advance how they will feel about, and react to, new developments because hunter-gatherers had no use for this ability.[155] Thus, natural selection did not favor those who were gifted in this regard.

Change was something that happened to our ancestors, not something they made happen. They lacked the tools and knowledge to reshape their environment to their liking, or to prevent unwanted developments from occurring. So their survival hinged not on effective long-term planning, but on adapting quickly and successfully to whatever came their way.

As we saw in Chapter 5 (page 106), because we are blessed with the ability to control so many aspects of our lives, we face a sometimes overwhelming array of choices. Unfortunately, when we contemplate options we have not yet experienced, our minds are prone to err by (1) **denying** a new development is headed our way, (2) **misjudging** how we are going to react when it arrives, and/or (3) **exaggerating** how happy or sad it will make us.

Denial

To protect their self-image, people often refuse to accept that an identity-threatening change can occur, will occur, or has occurred, despite strong evidence to the contrary. They insist, with unwavering confidence, that what must happen (continuity) will happen, and that what must not happen (change) will not or has not occurred.

This is unconscious self-promotion at work. As we saw in Chapter 3 (page 35), facts sometimes contradict a person's identity so flatly that no amount of spinning, bending, or twisting can preserve it. The only way someone can maintain a positive identity is by pretending these uncomfortable truths do not exist.

Short-term denial is neither an illness nor a failing. It provides the breathing space mentally healthy people often need to adjust to new circumstances.[156] We experience denial not only when dreaded changes occur, but also when dreams come true. Until the unconscious mind can mold a new positive identity, denial helps keep the old one in place.

Unfortunately, the breakneck speed of 21st century life often provides too little time to adjust. Opportunities leave the station before people recognize the need to hop on board.

Misjudging

When people gauge how they will behave in an unfamiliar situation, their estimates are often wildly off the mark. The reason is that, as we saw in Chapter 4 (page 63), the unconscious mind operates on experience. It predicts the future by comparing present circumstances to memories of similar events. Until an event occurs it is an idea, not a circumstance. So intuition indicates how we feel about the idea, not how the idea, should it come to pass, will make us feel.

The difference is critical because we react to ideas idealistically—by feeling the way we want to feel—whereas we react to reality realistically—by feeling the way we need to feel. This is why people often experience a sudden and profound "change of heart" when a moment of truth arrives and reality sets in. Common examples related to conflict include the following:

- Litigants who get cold feet as they climb the courthouse steps and suddenly decide to settle.

- Witnesses who have a "come to Jesus moment" (abruptly change their story) when they take the stand and place their hand on the Bible.

- Negotiators who have "second thoughts" when the time comes to formalize terms they said they would agree to.

- Parties who experience buyer's remorse shortly after signing an agreement and want to back out.

Reality may set in just before, during, or shortly after an event. And when it does, powerful new emotions prompt people to act in unexpected ways. They may suddenly resist what they have long supported, embrace what they have consistently opposed, come clean after repeatedly lying, or lie about what they have previously admitted.

Exaggerating

We frequently overestimate how happy or sad a change will make us feel and how long these positive or negative feelings will last.[157] The reason is simple: we fail to take into account the fact that, when circumstances change, we change right along with them.[158]

The unconscious mind adapts to change in three stages.

1. Developing a new concept of normality.

As we learned in Chapter 4 (page 65), the unconscious mind assumes that repetition equals reliability. The more a behavior repeats itself, the more confident we become that it will continue to recur. The focus in Chapter 4 was on how this rule of thumb occasionally leads intuition astray. The point here is that this rule defines what we think of as normal.

When a change first occurs, it strikes us as odd because it is different from what we are used to. But once a new pattern develops, we become accustomed to it and regard it as normal. Any deviation now seems abnormal.

2. Altering its sense of identity to accord with this new norm.

As we learned in Chapter 3 (page 19), nothing is more important for survival than maintaining an identity that enables you to enlist cooperation from the people whose support you need. When times change, you may need cooperation from a different group of people, or you may need to behave differently in order to maintain support from the same people. You must adjust accordingly.

When people develop a new identity, they alter their basis of comparison. A positive turn of events triggers an upgrade. A negative development prompts a downgrade. So, over time, a change that at first seems remarkably good or bad blends into the natural order of things and eventually seems merely fair.

3. Aligning memories with this new identity.

We also learned in Chapter 3 that the unconscious mind shapes memories to promote our identity. By extension, when our identity changes, we must bend, twist, or forget the past to the extent necessary to conform to the image we now want to project.[159]

In summary, before we have a chance to adapt, the only way we can cope with a major new development is to deny its existence. Once we make the necessary adjustments, the new circumstance starts to feel real. As time marches further on, we reshape memories to tell a positive story about how the change occurred and who we are now.[160] At this point, the change begins to seem inevitable. We cannot imagine how events possibly could have turned out any other way. Our minds have now come full circle. Once again, they hold a firm, fixed view of reality.[161]

PREDICTING THE UNPREDICTABLE

When anticipating reactions to new circumstances, we tend to assume not only that we will stay the same, but also that other aspects of our life will remain steady. Because this second assumption is as suspect as the first, it also helps explain why predicting emotions is so hazardous.

A simple example: Janet is excited about taking a job in a new city but thinks she will miss her old neighborhood a lot.

Scenario #1: While selling furniture in anticipation of the move, Janet falls madly in love with a man who comes by to check out an antique desk. Now, Janet is having second thoughts about moving.

Scenario #2: Shortly after the move, Janet's old neighborhood is ravaged by a hurricane and the house she had rented is seriously damaged. Janet now feels ecstatic about having relocated.

Whenever you try to anticipate how an expected change will make you feel, bear in mind that surprises will color your emotions in ways you cannot anticipate.

In the process, emotions triggered by a new development lose their charge. A novel event triggers strong positive or negative emotions—depending upon whether it is welcome or not. When the novelty wears off, there is no longer anything to get excited about. Once incorporated into the fabric of our everyday life, a previously remarkable event literally disappears from consciousness. As the simple shop, mop, top game (see "Three Is a Charm," page 65) illustrates, patterns that seem consistent attract no attention.

So once people adapt to a new development, they are generally about as happy or sad as they were beforehand. Only cataclysmic changes that exceed our capacity to adapt cause a lasting change in outlook.

BRANCHING OUT

Four years ago . . .

Municipal Bank was a family-owned corporation with fifteen branches in a small midwestern city. Derrick Junior, age sixty-five, began working for the bank right after college and took over as president when his father, the founder, retired thirty years ago.

Three large financial institutions, Consolidated, North American, and Coastal, are aggressively developing national banking networks by gobbling up or driving away local and regional banks. They focused initially on large metropolitan areas but have begun to infiltrate small cities.

Three years ago . . .

Amid rumors that the so-called Big Three are about to hit the Midwest "like a summer twister," Eric, the vice president of customer service, leaves Municipal for a position in new business development at Consolidated. Almost simultaneously, Coastal purchases Municipal's primary local competitor, First Bank of the Midwest.

Emilio, the executive vice president, had seen the handwriting on the wall before he joined Municipal two years ago. Although

Derrick has been grooming Emilio as his successor, Emilio believes his real future lies in orchestrating the sale of Municipal to a national chain, with a position for himself in the bargain. Emilio has been whispering in Derrick's ear about the need to sell for years. Now he feels the time has come to pump up the volume.

Emilio immediately promotes Rhonda, the youngest and least experienced branch manager, to fill Eric's vacant slot as VP for customer service. The announcement emphasizes Rhonda's creativity and flexibility, noting that, in times of rapid upheaval, these qualities trump experience.

The next week, Emilio bluntly informs Derrick that modernizing can only increase Municipal's sale price. Competing long-term with the lions at the gate is impossible. And once Municipal loses its customer base, it will be worthless.

Derrick tells Emilio just as bluntly that the merchants in this city would never abandon one of their own. When Emilio notes the demise of local supermarkets, pharmacies, and hardware stores, Derrick counters, "Banking is different ... more personal. And besides, I'm not ready to retire. What would I do all day?"

In the ensuing year ...

At first, her promotion seems too good to be true. Rhonda cannot believe she is really a vice president. How will she win the respect of the branch managers, her former colleagues? Some (or all) no doubt strongly resent her quick rise.

Emilio's words start to sink in: Rhonda's fresh ideas are indeed worth more than anyone's archaic experience. So Rhonda quickly asserts herself. She has the website redesigned to drive potential customers to their local branch. Then, she trains all branch employees to promote an expanded range of services at every opportunity. When these changes became part of Municipal's way of doing business, Rhonda can no longer imagine herself working as a branch manager under the old regime.

At the outset, the higher salary, greater perks, and bigger

office are a thrill. But once she acclimates to the rigors of being a vice president, Rhonda feels entitled to every penny she receives. Then, after accomplishing so much in her first year, Rhonda begins to resent being the lowest paid VP. When Emilio refuses to bump her compensation up to the midrange for VPs, Rhonda is incensed and threatens to start looking around.

Meanwhile . . .

Through Rotary Club connections, Emilio arranges for Derrick to meet with two former owners of family banks who sold their assets to a Big Three network. Derrick listens intently as Howard, who is now a business school professor, and Craig, who helps non-governmental organizations in Asia implement financial controls, recount how they finally came to terms with the need to sell. Both Howard and Craig go on at length about the excitement and rewards of their second career. Derrick tells Emilio that his "devious, underhanded plot succeeded."

Six months later . . .

Derrick and Emilio secure a deal to merge Municipal into North American. Emilio becomes a regional vice president.

One year ago . . .

A recession hits the financial industry hard. Emilio instructs all his direct reports, including Rhonda, to generate a plan for eliminating positions. Rhonda forwards this request to her branch managers. Steven recommends terminating his two newest employees, Anne and Roberta, rather than Sylvia, an eighty-year-old veteran with declining skills. When Rhonda presses for an explanation, Steven admits Sylvia is a bit past her prime but says he just doesn't have the heart to fire someone who has worked for him for twenty-five years, is just barely getting by, and will never find another job.

Rhonda angrily replies, "Fine. If you don't have the guts, I'll do it myself."

A week later, just as she is about to send her final layoff list to

Emilio, Rhonda deletes Sylvia's name and recommends that Roberta be axed instead.

Nine months ago . . .

The recession worsens, forcing North American to cut even more positions, including those of Rhonda and many other vice presidents. Since he regards Rhonda as his protégé, Emilio offers her first dibs on the only available slot: managing a branch in a neighboring state. Rhonda simply cannot fathom accepting a huge demotion, so she thanks Emilio but tells him she is certain something better will come along soon. Rhonda's pink slip arrives five days later.

Three months ago . . .

After six months of being unemployed and seeing almost no openings in the banking industry, Rhonda happily accepts an offer from Consolidated to manage a small, suburban branch office for half of what she had earned at North American. Since Rhonda is running out of money and knows a least a dozen former vice presidents who are still unemployed, she is grateful for the opportunity.

Shortly thereafter . . .

Before Rhonda begins working again, she fears that accepting orders from someone who used to be a peer will be humiliating. But Rhonda quickly casts this thought aside when she realizes how much Consolidated differs from North American. She convinces herself that, in the long run, coming in at a lower level, where she can learn the ropes while maintaining a low profile, will work to her advantage. So all is for the best.

The sale: At first, Derrick's wall of denial puts him into direct conflict with Emilio about the need to merge Municipal into a national chain. But Derrick comes around after he sees that, by pursuing a second career, he can develop a new positive identity. Emilio wisely recognizes the best way to convey this message to Derrick is through the experiences of men he regards as peers.

The promotion: How could a promotion lead to conflict? Because of how quickly and thoroughly Rhonda adapts to it. Immediately after she is promoted, Rhonda still thinks of herself as a branch chief, so vice-presidential pay seems like a windfall. And she is very grateful to Emilio for the opportunity. Once Rhonda begins to think of herself as a vice president, other vice presidents become her basis of comparison. Consequently, Rhonda feels entitled to her pay. After accomplishing so much in her first year, Rhonda starts to identify herself as a high-performing VP, and, therefore, resents being paid less than weaker performers. Rhonda's demand to surpass them triggers a dispute with Emilio.

The layoffs: Rhonda initiates a dispute with Steven because she misjudges how she would react to an unfamiliar situation (i.e., devastating an elderly widow). Rhonda has no relevant experience to draw from: she has terminated employees before, but only for strong cause. Enamored with the idea of being "tough" (which she defines as doing what is best for the bottom line regardless of the human toll), Rhonda imagines she would retain young employees with potential rather than Sylvia. She therefore berates Steven for his lack of courage. When reality sets in, however, the thought of letting Sylvia go makes Rhonda sick to her stomach and she relents.

The offer of a demotion: Because she is in denial about being laid off, Rhonda rejects an offer Emilio regards as extremely generous.

The new position: Rhonda emerges from six months of unemployment with a profoundly different sense of fairness. She still misses being a vice president, but she is now pleased just to have a job. Compared with other former vice presidents, most of whom are still out of work, Rhonda is a success. To promote her new identity, Rhonda creates a happy tale in which entering Consolidated in a lower-level position is a savvy career move.

CHANGE AND CONFLICT

Conventional wisdom holds that since people are inherently risk averse, they resist change. Hence, change leads to conflict. This is a very incomplete picture of how new developments affect human relationships.

Perceptions of Risk

Someone is risk averse if they are more strongly motivated to conserve what is already theirs than to acquire what they want but do not have. When weighing the advantages and disadvantages of a proposed change, a risk-averse person will overvalue potential losses and undervalue potential gains.

Since our paramount goal is survival, our minds urge us not to jeopardize our ability to meet basic needs. So when we have all we require, risking it to obtain something extra seems foolish. In dire straits, however, the calculus is just the opposite. Staying the course is suicidal. Taking huge risks is the only way to cope.[*]

So why do people remain in circumstances that seem oppressive or intolerable? The operative word is "seem." If you have never lived a certain way yourself, it may be impossible to fathom how someone could adjust to such conditions. Their normal way of life may strike you as an unthinkable nightmare. But to them it is okay, not because they are inherently risk-averse, but because they are inherently adaptable.

Perceptions of Change

Does change cause conflict? Yes, in the situations we notice, but not as a general rule. Changes that trigger serious disputes command our attention. Changes that neither cause friction nor ease tensions slip by

---

[*] An example from the author's personal experience: Like most people, under normal circumstances, I shy away from poison (aka chemotherapy) and radiation. But at age thirty-five, when I contracted acute myelogenous leukemia (AML), my risk calculus shifted 180 degrees overnight. If I refused treatment, I was certain to die in a matter of days. Treatment would afford me a 20–40 percent chance of surviving AML and would increase my risk of developing a potentially deadly solid cancer tumor by a much smaller amount. So I hastily signed the consent form. I did not shy away from risk. Nor did I embrace it. I just did what would help me survive.

largely or entirely unnoticed.

Imagine that the loss of a job causes a couple's income to plummet. Faced with very difficult decisions about how to make ends meet, they are likely to get into serious arguments that will command their attention both day and night. But when the situation turns around and the couple's income rises to new heights, how often will they say to each other: "Hey honey, remember how this decision would have triggered an argument three years ago? Isn't great how we are past that now?"

Changes are as likely to prevent or resolve problems as they are to trigger disputes. But, just as news programs feature what's wrong, not what's right, our minds are far more attuned to developments that produce ill effects.

SHAKING THINGS UP

Change is good because the mind thrives on stimulation. This is why boredom (a negative emotion) motivates us to seek new challenges and joy (a positive emotion) rewards us for figuring out how to overcome them.

BEST PRACTICES IN MANAGING CHANGE

Gaining Support from Others

1. Make It Real

We discover how a new development will affect us through experience, not from learning facts, figures, or concepts.

Direct, personal engagement is the best teacher.[162] Whenever possible, include the people whose cooperation you seek in a pilot test, a dry run, a demonstration project, a role play or some other hands-on activity that resembles or closely mimics the type of change you want them to support.

Witnessing or learning about the experiences of others is second best. For example, in "Branching Out" (page 138), Emilio arranged for Derrick to hear Howard and Craig describe their successful transitions from family bank president to a fulfilling second career.

Since the unconscious mind fails to distinguish fantasy from fact (see Chapter 4, page 83), a fictional enactment can have the desired impact. Imagine you are trying to convince wary physicians to convert to an electronic record-keeping system. You want to show how easy the system is to use, but for legal reasons you cannot use actual patient records. No problem. Fake but realistic-looking charts and notes will make the point just as well as the real thing.

2. Be Realistic

Expect and plan for opposition. No matter what degree of direct or indirect engagement you provide, people may not recognize in advance how quickly or successfully they will adapt to a significant new development. So expect overreaction and irrational resistance, and plan accordingly. For example, after you demonstrate to a group of physicians who have kept handwritten notes for thirty years that a new system is faster and more reliable, do not assume they will automatically embrace it. Create incentives for giving the system a try. Ask those who try and find they like it to speak with their peers. Continue to highlight the advantages of the new system, and the disadvantages of old way of doing things, through multiple forms of communication. Offer follow-up training and support.

Phase in change gradually. When a change threatens someone's identity, they will remain anxious until the threat disappears. One way to remove a threat is by combating it, but the fight is often futile. For example, in "Branching Out" (page 139), Rhonda is powerless to halt the recession that is causing widespread job cutbacks in the banking industry. The other response is to adapt. As we have seen, this takes time. In the interim, anxiety wears on both body and mind. So whenever possible, avoid making more than one major change at a time, and allow enough time after each disruption for a full recovery.

Judge cautiously. Unless you have actually walked a mile in the shoes you are asking others to wear, your natural inclination will be to judge them with reference to how you would hope to react (which you know), not how you would actually behave (which you do not know). Acknowledge that the gap between these two standards may be large, and proceed with humility.

3. Be Positive

Focus on gains, not losses. People assess fairness in relative terms, and there is often room for debate about what basis of comparison is appropriate (see Chapter 3, page 22). So pick a point of comparison that tells a positive story, one that frames the change you want others to embrace as a win for them.[163]

In "Branching Out" (page 139), when Emilio suggested that Rhonda downgrade to a branch manager position, she framed it as a huge loss. Six months later, she framed the same job offer as a lucky break. Whether a change is positive or negative is a matter of perspective.

4. Make It Happen

If you firmly believe a change will benefit others, do not hesitate to drag them kicking and screaming into the future—no matter how fiercely they resist. Their attitude will change once they adapt. Eventually, they may even thank you.

When Someone Else Seeks Your Cooperation

When others want you to support a proposed change, respond based on your values, not your emotions. In other words, do what you think is right, not what you think will make you happier. Why? Because once you adapt, your overall outlook on life is likely to be about the same either way. But remaining true to your beliefs will make you feel a lot better about yourself.

CHAPTER EIGHT

HAPPINESS

People who need people are the luckiest people
in the world.

– Julie Styne and Bob Merrill
(from the musical *Funny Girl*)

Conflict resolution is not for the faint of heart—or mind. Implementing the best practices set forth in this book requires three traits that do not come easily:

- **Humility:** Our minds are inherently imperfect, and are easily confused and overwhelmed by many aspects of 21st century life. As a result, we must acknowledge and accept that our perceptions, beliefs, and memories may be inaccurate, and our emotions may be inappropriate. Believing that what you see, hear, feel, and remember is real is comforting. Abandoning that belief is unnerving.

- **Perseverance:** Blindly following your mental autopilot is easy. Steering a different course—straight into strong emotional headwinds— is draining. Depending upon how a dispute unfolds, you may need to exercise an enormous amount of emotional restraint for short periods of time, maintain steady control over the long haul, or do a combination of both.

- **Courage:** Most disputes can be resolved cooperatively. They involve differences in perception, misunderstandings triggered by poor or insufficient communication, or substantive gaps that can be bridged through compromise or collaboration. But some differences are irreconcilable: no mutually acceptable solution is available. In addition, parties often fail to reach agreement even when the gap between them can be breached. Best practices increase your chances of success, but they do not guarantee it. A critical factor, the other party's behavior, lies beyond your control.[164] So when you set out on the road to resolution, you must be willing to devote skill and energy to a potentially failing cause. That takes guts.

So the ultimate question is, Why bother? The answer lies in one of the great challenges of 21st century life: finding happiness in the midst of plenty. Two aspects of the human mind we have already examined complicate this quest. The first is how quickly and thoroughly we adapt to change. The novelty of a new house, car, boat, wardrobe, or lover wears off quickly, and with it goes the sense of excitement. The second is that, because our minds are geared for survival, not pleasure, negative emotions predominate. We feel bad for however long a need remains unaddressed. When it is finally met, we enjoy only a brief period of pleasure before other unmet needs clamor for attention.

Close personal relationships are an exception. Since our ancestors' survival hinged on maintaining strong bonds throughout their lifetime, success in this realm provides continuous pleasure. Confidence that others will be there to support you when you need them is not thrilling or scintillating, but it sure is comforting.

Unfortunately, no matter how compatible two people are, they cannot intertwine their professional or personal lives for any length of time without experiencing conflict. Perceptions and interests are never perfectly aligned. We all have different views and objectives.

Our ancestors made whatever sacrifices were necessary to sustain key relationships because their survival hung in the balance. Today, however, failure is often regarded as an option. People feel they can address professional disputes by finding a different job, replacing a business partner, or recruiting a new employee. On the personal side, we can terminate relationships with spouses, partners, friends, and relatives because all the goods and services required to live well and raise children are available for purchase. Intimacy is now discretionary, easily replaced by income and investments.

Thus, as prosperity has increased, clans and multigenerational households have broken down into nuclear families, and many nuclear families have splintered into single-person and single-parent households. Simultaneously, longstanding business partnerships and career-long employment relationships have dissolved into a stream of "human capital" that flows from one short-term opportunity to another.

So, while forming new casual relationships has never been easier, thanks in particular to the Internet, forging and sustaining close bonds has never been harder. Every long-standing relationship gets tarnished by anger, resentment, jealousy, and daily annoyances. With shiny new replacements within easy reach, people often question whether polishing the old ones off is worth the effort. Is the joy and comfort that strong ties bring worth the humility, perseverance, and courage they demand in return?[166] In the 21st century, you get to choose.

EARTHLY PLEASURE

A Gallup World Poll conducted in 2005–2006 measured the relationship between wealth and happiness.[165] Conducted in 132 nations with a combined total of 96 percent of the world's population, it was the first representative sampling of the entire human population.

Part 1 tracked happiness on three fronts:

- How respondents ranked their life on a scale of 0 (worst possible) to 10 (best possible)

- Whether respondents had recently experienced positive feelings (enjoyment, smiling, or laughing)

- Whether respondents had recently experienced negative feelings (worry, sadness, depression, or anger)

Part 2 gathered data on two possible predictors of happiness: economic wealth, measured by personal and national income, and social psychological wealth, measured by whether the respondent was experiencing the following:

- learning new things

- making good use of skills

- respect   →

→ • family or friends he or she could count on in an emergency

  • free choice in how he or she spent time

Life evaluations strongly correlated with personal and national income. Rich people in prosperous societies felt they were living the best possible life. Poor people in destitute nations felt just the opposite.

Positive and negative emotions correlated strongly with social psychological factors—and only weakly with income. People who felt respected, supported, empowered, and so on experienced joy even if their income was modest. People who felt disrespected, abandoned, or misused experienced worry, sadness, anger, or depression even if their income was high.

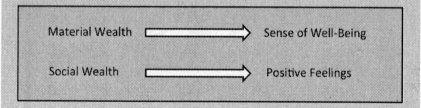

The United States ranked #1 in income but below the middle in negative feelings, whereas some countries in Central America and Africa scored higher on social wealth than economic prosperity. A few countries scored near the top on all scales, proving that material and social wealth can happily coexist.

NOTES

Preface

[1] Matt Ridley, *The Red Queen: Sex and the Evolution of Human Nature* (London: Viking, 1993), 10.

[2] Ridley, *The Red Queen,* 10–11.

[3] Maya Angelou, "The Human Family," *The Complete Collected Poems of Maya Angelou,* (New York: Random House, 1994), 225.

1. Key Terms

[4] Jesse S.Nirenberg, *Getting through to People* (Englewood Cliffs, NJ: Prentice-Hall, 1963), 67.

2. How the Human Mind Works: A Brief Overview

[5] Daniel Goleman, *Emotional Intelligence* (New York: Bantam Books, 1995), 6.

[6] Gerd Gigerenzer, *Gut Feelings: The Intelligence of the Unconscious* (New York: Penguin 2007), 210.

[7] Michael Tomasello, *Why We Cooperate* (Cambridge, MA: MIT Press, 2009), ix–x.

[8] Martin A. Nowak, *SuperCooperators: Altruism, Evolution, and Why We Need Each Other to Succeed* (New York: Free Press, 2011), xii.

[9] James A. Estes et al.," Trophic Downgrading of Planet Earth," *Science* 333, no. 6040 (July 15, 2011): 301–06, doi: 10.1126/science.1205106. This symbiotic relationship between predator and prey is part of a larger scheme of cooperation that promotes a sustainable environment. When predators are extinguished, soaring numbers of prey animals such as elk and deer gobble up vegetation, depleting fields and forests.

[10] Daniel Goleman, *Social Intelligence: The New Science of Human Relationships* (New York: Bantam Books, 2006), 131.

[11] Albert Mehrabian, "Communication without Words," *Psychology Today* 2 (1968): 52–55. Furthermore, people find visual and vocal cues more credible because they are harder to fake. A study revealed that, on average, 55 percent of communication about emotions occurs through facial expressions and body language (visual cues); 38 percent through

intonation and inflection (vocal cues), and just 7 percent through words (verbal cues). See note 48 below.

[12] Leslie A. Hart, *How the Brain Works: A New Understanding of Human Learning, Emotion, and Thinking* (New York: Basic Books, 1975), 173.

[13] Antonio R. Damasio, *Descartes' Error: Emotion, Reason, and The Human Brain* (New York: G.P. Putnam, 1994), 192–95.

[14] Goleman, *Emotional Intelligence*, 294.

[15] Joseph LeDoux, *Synaptic Self: How Our Brains Become Who We Are* (New York: Viking, 2001), 323. "*Doing* the right thing doesn't always flow naturally from *knowing* what the right thing to do is."

3. Identity

[16] Guy Gugliotta, "And the Extended Life Span Goes to . . . the Oscar Winner!," *Washington Post* (March 1, 2006), A2. Even in modern society, higher social status correlates with an increased life span. For example, actors and actresses who receive an Academy Award (Oscar) live 3.9 years longer, on average, than unsuccessful nominees.

[17] Douglas H. Yarn and Gregory Todd Jones, "In Our Bones (Or Brains): Behavioral Biology," in *The Negotiator's Fieldbook,* ed. Andrea K. Schneider and Christopher Honeyman (Washington, DC: American Bar Association, Section of Dispute Resolution, 2006), 283–91.

[18] Gigerenzer, *Gut Feelings*, 53.

[19] "A Rising Tide?," *The Washington Post* (March 12, 2006): B6. When asked whether they would prefer to earn $100,000 in a society in which the average pay is $80,000, or $130,000 in which the average pay is $110,000, most people pick the lower salary. Being relatively rich (better than average) takes priority over being absolutely rich (earning more money).

[20] Victoria H. Medvec, Scott F. Madley and Thomas Gilovich, "When Less Is More: Counterfactual Thinking and Satisfaction Among Olympic Athletes," *Journal of Personality and Social Psychology* 69, no. 4 (1995): 603–10. For example, bronze medalists at the Olympics tend to be happier than silver medalists because the former feel lucky to have gotten a medal whereas the latter obsess about what they could have done to win. In other words, third place finishers tend to compare themselves to non-medalists, whereas second place finishers tend to compare themselves to gold medalists.

[21] Robert Axelrod, *The Evolution of Cooperation* (New York: Basic Books, 1984), viii–ix.

[22] "The Golden Rule," Wikipedia, accessed August 4, 2011, http://en.wikipedia.org /wiki/The_Golden_Rule_(ethics).

[23] Galatians 6:7 (KJV).

[24] Ridley, *The Red Queen,* 332.

[25] Yarn and Jones, "In Our Bones (or Brains)," 287.

[26] David A. Fahrenthold, "It's Natural to Behave Irrationally," *The Washington Post* (December 8, 2009), E1. A 2007 study measured the impact of door flyers on energy conversation. Flyers that emphasized helping the environment, social responsibility, and saving money induced less conservation than flyers that said the majority of neighbors in the community were conserving. The point: being "good" is an abstract sense is not as important to people as reciprocating what peers have done.

[27] Gigerenzer, *Gut Feelings*, 211.

[28] David G. Myers, *Intuition: Its Powers and Perils* (New Haven, CT: Yale University Press, 2002), 94–97.

[29] Goleman, *Social Intelligence*, 109.

[30] Kevin K. Walsh and Robert Deitchman, "Evaluation of Early Childhood Programs: The Role of Parents," *Child Care Quarterly* 9, no. 4 (1980): 289–98.

[31] Daniel Kahneman, J. L. Knetsch, and R. H. Thaler, "Experimental Tests of the Endowment Effect and the Coase Theorem," *Journal of Political Economy* 98 (1990): 1325–48.

[32] Simone Moran and Maurice Schweitzer, "When Better Is Worse: Envy and the Use of Deception in Negotiations," *Negotiation & Conflict Management Research* 1, no. 11 (2008): 3–29.

[33] Glynis M. Breakwell, *Coping with Threatened Identities* (London: Methuen, 1986), 87. The ultimate form of denial occurs when people feel compelled to act contrary to firmly held beliefs. They perceive themselves leaving their body and entering a different realm, and they recall the incident as if it happened to someone else.

[34] *Washington Post* telephone survey of 1,033 randomly selected adults conducted Nov. 4–8, 2005, by ICR Research of Media, Pennsylvania.

[35] Kaja Perina, "Love's Loopy Logic," *Psychology Today* (January 1, 2007), last reviewed February 1, 2011, http://www.psychologytoday.com/articles/200612/loves-loopy-logic (citing research conducted by Faby Gagne' and John Lydon). The flip side, of course, is that opinions of ex-lovers tend to be negative.

[36] Ulrike Malmendier and Geoffrey Tate, "CEO Overconfidence and Corporate Investment," *The Journal of Finance* 60, no. 6 (December 2006): 2661–2700.

[37] Daniel Kahneman and Amos Tversky, *Choices, Values, and Frames* (New York: Russell Sage Foundation, 2000), 161.

[38] Daniel Kahneman and Amos Tversky, "Conflict Resolution: A Cognitive Perspective," in *Barriers to Conflict Resolution*, ed. Kenneth Arrow et al. (New York: W.W. Norton, 1995), 47–48.

[39] Robert H. Mnookin, Scott R. Peppet, and Andrew S. Tulumello, *Beyond Winning: Negotiating to Create Value in Deals and Disputes* (Cambridge, MA: Belknap Press, 2000), 34.

[40] Kahneman and Tversky, "Conflict Resolution: A Cognitive Perspective," 49.

[41] Mnookin et al., *Beyond Winning,* 52.

[42] Robert Trivers, "Reciprocal Altruism: 30 Years Later," in *Cooperation in Primates and Humans: Mechanisms and Evolution*, ed. C. P. van Schaik and P. M. Kappeler (Berlin: Springer-Verlag, 2005), 67–83.

[43] Carol Tavris and Elliot Aronson, *Mistakes Were Made (but Not by Me): Why We Justify Foolish Beliefs, Bad Decisions, and Hurtful Acts* (Orlando, FL: Harcourt, 2007), 9.

[44] Tavris and Aronson, *Mistakes Were Made (but Not by Me)*, 6. When husbands and wives were asked to estimate the percentage of housework they perform the answers generally total significantly more than 100 percent. *Negotiation* 14, no. 4 (April, 2011): 4. When authors of research papers were asked to estimate their contribution to the final product, the average total for a team of four was 140 percent. Similarly, joint-venture partners routinely overestimate their contribution to an alliance's success.

[45] Robert Trivers, "The Elements of a Scientific Theory of Self-Deception," *Annals of New York Academy of Sciences* 907 (2000): 114–31.

[46] Gigenenzer, *Gut Feelings*, 60.

[47] Damasio, *Descartes' Error*, 142.

[48] Albert Mehrabian, *Silent Messages* (Belmont, CA: Wadsworth, 1971), iii.

[49] Tavris and Aronson, *Mistakes Were Made (but Not by Me)*, 26–27. Harm can trigger a

"vicious cycle" in which the wrongdoer justifies his actions by finding reasons to blame the victim.

[50] Tavris and Aronson, *Mistakes Were Made (but Not by Me)*, 60. Thoughts determine actions, but the reverse is also true. To a very significant extent, our minds shape thoughts to conform to our actions.

[51] Tavris and Aronson, *Mistakes Were Made (but Not by Me)*, 28. Aid can trigger a "virtuous cycle" in which the helper justifies his actions by identifying positive qualities in the people he assisted.

[52] Myers, *Intuition*, 100.

[53] Randall L. Kiser, "Let's Not Make a Deal: An Empirical Study of Decision-Making in Unsuccessful Settlement Negotiations," *Journal of Empirical Legal Studies* 5 (September 2008): 551–91. An exhaustive study conducted over a forty-four-year period found that plaintiffs who reject settlement offers end up doing no better or worse at trial 61 percent of the time. Defendants who reject offers and go to trial do no better or worse only 21–24 percent of time, but their mistakes are far more consequential. The average verdict is twenty-six times the plaintiff's last offer.

[54] Nowak, *Supercooperators*, xi–xv.

[55] Goleman, *Social Intelligence*, 231.

[56] Naomi I. Eisenberger, Matthew D. Lieberman, and Kipling D. Williams, "Does Rejection Hurt? An MRI Study of Social Exclusion," *Science* 302, no. 5643 (October 10, 2003): 290–92, doi: 10.1126/science.1089134. Neuroimaging reveals that social exclusion activates the same region of the brain as physical pain.

[57] Alberto Melucci, *The Playing Self: Person and Meaning in the Planetary Society* (Cambridge: Cambridge University Press, 1996), 31.

[58] Breakwell, *Coping with Threatened Identities*, 40–41.

[59] Louis Kriesberg, *The Sociology of Social Conflicts* (Englewood Cliffs, NJ: Prentice-Hall, 1973), 163.

[60] Scott Plous, *The Psychology of Judgment and Decision Making* (Philadelphia: Temple University Press, 1993), 252.

[61] Douglas Stone, Bruce Satton, and Sheila Heen, *Difficult Conversations: How to Discuss What Matters Most* (New York: Penguin Books, 2000), 114. Complex and mixed identities are more capable of incorporating input without having to distort, reject, or be devastated by it.

[62] Shankar Vedantam, "The Christmastime Self-Esteem Paradox," *Washington Post* (December 10, 2007), A3. To be effective, reframing must be perceived as honest. People accept characterizations that accord with, or are slightly more favorable than, their self-image. But feedback that seems inauthentic makes people feel misunderstood.

[63] Mnookin et al., *Beyond Winning*, 17.

[64] Kahneman and Tversky, "Conflict Resolution: A Cognitive Perspective," 46.

[65] Breakwell, *Coping with Threatened Identities*, 111.

[66] Robert H. Mnookin and Less Ross, "Introduction," in *Barriers to Conflict Resolution*, ed. Kenneth Arrow et al. (New York: W.W. Norton, 1995), 22.

[67] Shankar Vedantam, "Spending More for a Little Solace," *Washington Post* (August 27, 2007), A3. People frequently purchase goods and services not only to enjoy them, but also because they confer social status.

[68] Dean F. Griffen et al., Violations of Behavioral Practices Revealed in Closed Claims Reviews," *Annals of Surgery*, 248, no 3 (September 2008): 468–74.

[69] Scott Atran and Robert Axelrod, "Reframing Sacred Values," *Negotiation Journal* (July 2008): 221–46. Values are not always fungible. For example, when a dispute threatens "sacred values" (ideas that lie at the core of how people identify themselves), an offer of material compensation is likely to be regarded as an insult. However, a symbolic gesture of no material worth that conveys respect for these values may be well received.

[70] Nirenberg, *Getting through to People*, 167.

[71] Trivers, *Reciprocal Altruism*, 82.

[72] Michael E. McCullough, *Beyond Revenge: The Evolution of the Forgiveness Instinct* (San Francisco: Jossey-Bass, 2008), 183–84.

[73] Ridley, *The Red Queen*, 204–5. In one carefully studied traditional society, two-thirds of the inhabitants who made it to age forty had lost a close relative to murder.

[74] Maria W. Merritt, John M. Doris, and Gilbert Harman, "Character," in *The Moral Psychology Handbook,* ed. John M. Doris and the Moral Psychology Research Group (Oxford, UK: Oxford University Press, 2010), 390. With regard to public policy, the thirst to right wrongs has the opposite effect. Problems that create relatively minor consequences, but for which a person or group is clearly to blame, command disproportionately more attention and resources than "Acts of God" such as fires, floods, and outbreaks of disease. If saving lives was our only concern, we would do better to spend public funds on preventing diabetes instead of combatting terrorism. But the desire to punish evildoers often takes priority.

[75] John Dalberg-Acton, letter to Bishop Mandell Creighton, 5 April 1887.

4. Intuition

[76] Myers, Intuition, 40.

[77] Hart, *How the Brain Works,* 63. These feelings are often referred to as "gut reactions" or "heartfelt opinions" because they trigger sensations in the torso. However, all emotions emanate from the unconscious mind.

[78] Hart, *How the Brain Works,* 168.

[79] Lewis Carroll, "The Hunting of the Snark" (1876), 3.

[80] Robert B. Cialdini, *Influence: The Psychology of Persuasion* (New York: William Morrow, 1995), 191.

[81] Gigerenzer, *Gut Feelings,* 82–85.

[82] Gigerenzer, *Gut Feelings,* 8 and 195; Plous, *The Psychology of Judgment and Decision Making,* 109–10.

[83] Goleman, *Emotional Intelligence,* 20.

[84] Hart, *How the Brain Works,* 96.

[85] Cialdini, *Influence,* 116.

[86] Colin J. Davis, Jeffrey S. Bowers, and Amina Memon, Social Influence in Televised Election Debates: A Potential Distortion of Democracy. PLoS ONE (March 30, 2011 6(3): e18154 doi:10.1371/journal.pone.0018154.

[87] Lee Ross, "Reactive Devaluation in Negotiation and Conflict Resolution," in *Barriers to Conflict Resolution,* ed. Kenneth Arrow et al. (New York: W.W. Norton, 1995), 30–31.

[88] Shankar Vedantam, "Good Options Can Mask Bad Choices," *The Washington Post* (January 14, 2008), A3. People who have the luxury of deciding between two very attractive options (such as spending a surplus) are regarded as wiser than people who confront difficult choices between unpleasant options.

[89] Sophocles, *Oedipus Rex*, line 277.

[90] Nirenberg, *Getting Through to People*, 157.

[91] Gigerenzer, *Gut Feelings*, 50.

[92] Robert H. Mnookin and Lee Ross, "Introduction," 15. The tendency of parties in conflict to reflexively devalue ideas advanced by the other side is a major barrier to reaching agreements.

[93] See note 35.

[94] Gigerenzer, *Gut Feelings*, 8.

[95] Plous, *The Psychology of Judgment and Decision Making*, 234–35.

[96] Myers, *Intuition*, 118. Thus, "once beliefs form it can take more compelling evidence to change them than it did to create them."

[97] Myers, *Intuition*, 73. The Talmud states, "We don't see things as they are. We see things as we are."

[98] Plous, *The Psychology of Judgment and Decision Making*, 121.

[99] Goleman, *Social Intelligence*, 43. We sense emotions by feeling what others feel, not by analyzing their cues.

[100] Gigerenzer, *Gut Feelings*, 64. The conventional wisdom is that women are more "intuitive" than men in this regard, i.e., better able to read emotions. Some studies confirm this belief (Goleman, *Emotional Intelligence*, 97); some refute it (Gigerenzer, *Gut Feelings*, 71–73). Since people pay more attention to the emotions of others when they feel vulnerable (Goleman, *Social Intelligence*, 24), and women commonly perceive themselves as more vulnerable than men, the difference may lie in inclination rather than natural ability.

[101] Gigerenzer, *Gut Feelings*, 208.

[102] Nirenberg, *Getting through to People*, 67.

[103] Goleman, *Social Intelligence*, 14 and 39. People are most attentive to the emotions of others when they are afraid. We rely on each other to serve as sentinels of danger.

[104] Adam D. Galinsky, D. H. Gruenfeld, and J. C. Magee, "From Power to Action," *Journal of Personality and Social Psychology* 85 (2003): 453–66. People in positions of power are especially likely to ignore the feelings of subordinates in making decisions. They have more important matters on their mind.

[105] Gigerenzer, *Gut Feelings*, 15–16.

[106] Myers, *Intuition*, 34.

[107] Goleman, *Emotional Intelligence*, 291.

[108] Gigerenzer, *Gut Feelings*, 17.

[109] Gigerenzer, *Gut Feelings*, 31. The conscious mind can hold between five and eight items in short-term (working) memory at one time. This limits the number of facts or options that can be compared or contrasted.

[110] Hart, *How the Brain Works*, 138.

[111] Ap Dijksterhuis, Maarten W. Bos, Loran F. Nordgren, and Rick B. van Baaren, "On Making the Right Choice: The Deliberation-without-Attention Effect," *Science* 5763 (2006): 1006–8, doi 10.112/Science.1121629.

[112] Goleman, *Social Intelligence*, 86.

[113] Shankar Vedantam, "See No Bias," *The Washington Post* (January 23, 2005), W12.

[114] Ebonya Washington, "Female Socialization: How Daughters Affect Their Legislator Fathers' Voting on Women's Issues," *American Economic Review* 98, no. 1 (2008): 311–32.

[115] Vedantam, "See No Bias," W12; Goleman, *Social Intelligence*, 303. Contact with

members of other racial or ethnic groups (e.g., living in the same neighborhood) does not appear to reduce bias, but close personal friendships may make people less biased.

[116] Marianne Betrand and Sendhil Mullianathan, "Are Emily and Greg More Employable Than Lakisha and Jamal? A Field Experiment on Labor Market Discrimination," *American Economic Review* 94 (September 2004): 991–1013.

[117] Myers, *Intuition*, 196.

[118] Plous, *The Psychology of Judgment and Decision Making*, 237–38.

[119] Vedantam, "See No Bias," W12.

[120] David Hekman et. al, "An Examination of Whether and How Racial and Gender Biases Influence Customer Satisfaction," *Academy of Management Journal* 53, no. 2 (2010): 238–64. The minorities studied were Asian, African, and Latino.

[121] Vedantam, "See No Bias," W12.

[122] Ross, "Reactive Devaluation in Negotiation and Conflict Resolution," 27–29.

[123] Cialdini, *Influence*, 116–17.

[124] Chris Guthrie, Jeffrey J. Rachlinski, and Andrew J. Wistrich, "Inside the Judicial Mind," *Cornell University Law Review* 86 (2001): 787–92.

[125] See, e.g., Federal Rule of Evidence No. 408.

[126] Dan Orr and Chris Guthrie, "Anchoring, Information, Expertise, and Negotiation: New Insights from Meta-Analysis," *Ohio State Journal on Dispute Resolution* 21, no. 3 (2006): 623, http://papers.ssrn.com/sol3/papers.cfm?abstract_id=900152.

[127] Kathleen Kelley Reardon, *The Skilled Negotiator: Mastering the Language of Engagement* (San Francisco: Jossey-Bass, 2004), 32.

[128] Amos Tversky and Daniel Kahneman, "Judgment under Uncertainty: Heuristics and Biases," *Science* 185 (1974), 1124–30.

[129] Plous, *The Psychology of Judgment and Decision Making*, 240.

[130] Myers, *Intuition*, 118–19.

5. Reason

[131] Goleman, *Emotional Intelligence*, 28.

[132] David Hume, *A Treatise of Human Nature*, bk. 2, sect. 3 (Ithaca, NY: Cornell University Press, 2009), 286. "Reason is and ought only to be the slave of passions, and can never pretend to any other office than to serve and obey them."

[133] Barry Schwartz, *The Paradox of Choice: Why More Is Less*, (New York: Ecco, 2004), 151–52; Damasio, *Descartes' Error*, 229.

[134] Gigerenzer, *Gut Feelings*, 47.

[135] Schwartz, *Paradox of Choice*, 163; Melucci, *Playing Self*, 45. Choosing is stressful even when all options are attractive (e.g., one gourmet restaurant or another) because every road not taken is a foregone opportunity. Imagining what would have happened had we chosen a different path triggers regret.

[136] Goleman, *Emotional Intelligence*, 52.

[137] Nirenberg, *Getting through to People*, 170.

6. Anxiety

[138] Goleman, *Social Intelligence*, 272. What distinguishes an invigorating challenge from an unnerving threat is the perception of control. The tipping point is when a situation begins to feel overwhelming.

[139] "Anxiety," Wikipedia, accessed August 5, 2011, http://en.wikipedia.org/wiki/Anxiety; "Fight-or-Flight Response," Wikipedia, accessed August 5, 2011, http://en.wikipedia.org/wiki/Fight-or-flight_response.

[140] Goleman, *Emotional Intelligence*, 60–61.

[141] Goleman, *Social Intelligence*, 268.

[142] Goleman, *Emotional Intelligence*, 80.

[143] Hart, *How the Brain Works*, 125–28.

[144] Goleman, *Emotional Intelligence*, 136. Expressions of contempt or disgust, whether expressed verbally or through nonverbal cues, trigger the strongest reaction because they directly attack someone's identity.

[145] Sheldon D. Sheps, "Can Anxiety Increase Blood Pressure?," Mayo Clinic, accessed August 4, 2011, http://www.mayoclinic.com/health/anxiety/AN01086.

[146] Goleman, *Emotional Intelligence*, 172–73.

[147] "Sleep Debt," Wikipedia, accessed August 4, 2011, http://en.wikipedia.org/wiki/Sleep_debt.

[148] See note 141.

[149] Goleman, *Social Intelligence*, 277.

[150] Gerardo Ramirez, "Writing about Testing Worries Boosts Exam Performance in the Classroom," *Science* 331 (2011): 211. doi: 10.1126/science.1199427.

7. Change

[151] Eduardo B. Andrade and Dan Ariely, "The Enduring Impact of Transient Emotions on Decision Making," *Organizational Behavior and Human Decision Processes* 109 (2009): 1, 7.

[152] Goleman, *Emotional Intelligence*, 146.

[153] Michale Wohl and Nyla Branscombe, "Remembering Historical Victimization: Collective Guilt for Current Ingroup Transgressions," *Journal of Personality and Social Psychology* 94 (2008): 988–1006. Merely being reminded about an event that occurred long ago can trigger strong emotions that affect thinking about unrelated events. For example, after listening to a recap of the Japanese attack on Pearl Harbor in 1941, Americans felt less responsible for harm caused to Iraqi citizens by the 2003 invasion.

[154] Jennifer S. Lerner, "Negotiating under the Influence," *Negotiation* 6, no. 8 (June 2005): 1–3.

[155] Schwartz, *Paradox of Choice, 174.*

[156] Breakwell, *Coping with Threatened Identities*, 159–62.

[157] Myers, *Intuition*, 79–82.

[158] Schwartz, *Paradox of Choice*, 179.

[159] Howard Gardner, *Changing Minds: The Art and Science of Changing Our Own and Other People's Minds* (Boston: Harvard Business School Press, 2006), 185.

[160] Tavris and Aronson, *Mistakes Were Made (but Not by Me)*, 72–94; LeDoux, *Synaptic self*, 132.

[161] Gigerenzer, *Gut Feelings*, 19 (quoting Louis Agassiz: "First people say it conflicts with the Bible. Next, they say it has been discovered before. Lastly, they say they have always believed it.")

[162] Timothy D. Wilson, *Strangers to Ourselves: Discovering the Adaptive Unconscious* (Cambridge, MA: Belknap Press, 2002), 212. "One of the most enduring lessons of social

psychology is that behavior change often precedes changes in attitude and feelings."

[163] David Brooks, *The Social Animal* (New York: Random House, 2011), 181. If a surgeon advises a patient that a procedure has a 15 percent failure rate, the patient is likely to decide against it. If a surgeon characterizes the same procedure as having an 85 percent success rate, the patient is likely to consent.

8. Happiness

[164] The way we behave may influence how others behave toward us (Goleman, *Emotional Intelligence*, 115), but we cannot dictate their actions.

[165] Ed Diener, Weiting Ng, James Harter, and Raksha Arora, "Wealth and Happiness across the World: Material Prosperity Predicts Life Evaluation, Whereas Psychosocial Prosperity Predicts Positive Feeling," *Journal of Personality and Social Psychology* 99, no. 1 (2010): 52–61, doi: 10.1037/a0018066.

[166] James A. Coan, Hillary S. Schaefer, and Richard J. Davidson, "Lending a Hand: Social Regulation of the Neural Response to Threat," *Psychological Science* 17, no. 12 (2006): 1032–39. See also Goleman, *Emotional Intelligence*, 178. In making your decision, bear in mind that social ties have beneficial effects on health. Married people are, on average, healthier and happier than unmarried people. People in happy marriages are less likely to succumb to an infection and more likely to recovery quickly from an injury. Thus, social isolation is regarded as a major health risk.

INDEX